I Could Not Do Otherwise

I Could Not Do Otherwise

THE REMARKABLE LIFE OF DR. MARY EDWARDS WALKER

SARA LATTA

ZEST BOOKS
MINNEAPOLIS

This book is dedicated to those who have the courage to be true to themselves, even when the world makes it difficult.

Zest Books™
An imprint of Lerner Publishing Group, Inc.
241 First Avenue North
Minneapolis, MN 55401 USA

For reading levels and more information, look up this title at www.lernerbooks.com.
Visit us at zestbooks.net. 🅵 🅱

Designed by Athena Currier.

Main body text set in Janson Text LT Std.
Typeface provided by Adobe Systems.

Library of Congress Cataloging-in-Publication Data

Names: Latta, Sara L., author.
Title: I could not do otherwise: the remarkable life of Dr. Mary Edwards Walker / Sara Latta.
Description: Minneapolis: Zest Books, [2022] | Includes bibliographical references and index. | Audience: Ages 13–18 | Audience: Grades 10–12 | Summary: "This book explores the extraordinary life and work of Mary Edwards Walker, a Civil War surgeon, a spy captured by the Confederacy, and the only woman to have ever been awarded the Medal of Honor" —Provided by publisher.
Identifiers: LCCN 2021050546 (print) | LCCN 2021050547 (ebook) | ISBN 9781728413914 (library binding) | ISBN 9781728413921 (paperback) | ISBN 9781728445489 (ebook)
Subjects: LCSH: Walker, Mary Edwards, 1832–1919—Juvenile literature. | Women physicians—United States—Biography—Juvenile literature. | Physicians—United States—Biography. | Suffragists—United States—Biography—Juvenile literature. | United States—History—Civil War, 1861–1865—Medical care—Juvenile literature.
Classification: LCC R154.W18 L38 2022 (print) | LCC R154.W18 (ebook) | DDC 610.92 [B]—dc23/eng/20220111

LC record available at https://lccn.loc.gov/2021050546
LC ebook record available at https://lccn.loc.gov/2021050547

Manufactured in the United States of America
1-48561-49044-5/24/2022

CONTENTS

Mary Edwards Walker was proud to proclaim that she had never worn a corset in her lifetime. Instead, she wore a variety of styles including a knee-length skirt over trousers.

PROLOGUE

ON JUNE 27, 1865, JUST TWO MONTHS after the end of the
Civil War (1861–1865), the citizens of Richmond, Virginia,
were astonished to see a white woman in her mid-thirties walking down Broad Street dressed in a modified soldier's uniform.
She wore a blue coat with military buttons, a knee-length skirt
and, in the words of one journalist, a pair of "nicely-fitting blue
pants (not like the dandies now wear), and gaiters, which fitted
so as to display a pretty foot."

The sight of a woman dressed in military attire was shocking and would have attracted attention anywhere, but Dr. Mary
Edwards Walker, a surgeon for the Union army, was already
notorious in this southern city. A year earlier, she had been
captured by the Confederate army in Tennessee as a suspected
Union spy and spent time in the Castle Thunder Prison in
Richmond. Castle Thunder housed some of the "most dangerous prisoners" in the South: spies, deserters from the Confederate army, political prisoners, and people charged with treason. Once in Confederate hands, she was routinely ridiculed by
her captors and the local press for her clothing, her outspoken

manner, and her fervent belief in the emancipation of Black Americans. One of her Confederate captors wrote,

> *We were all amused and disgusted too at the sight of such a thing that nothing but the debased and depraved Yankee nation could produce—"a female doctor." . . . She was dressed in the full uniform of a Federal Surgeon, looks hat & all, & wore a cloak. . . . [She is] fair, not good looking and of course had tongue enough for a regiment of men.*

By June of 1865 the war was over, and Mary was a free woman again. She was seeking her brother, Alvah Jr., who had also served in the Union army. As she passed the splendid Powhatan House Hotel, she gained an impressive following of curious boys and girls. Gentlemen stared and shook their heads in dismay. Ladies, fashionably attired in tightly laced corsets and long, heavy skirts, stopped to gape and gossip at the strange woman.

At the corner of Sixth and Broad Streets, a military guard stopped her. "What authority," he asked, "do you have to appear on the streets in such outlandish garb?"

"By what authority do you make the inquiry?" Mary replied.

"By order of the Provost Marshall," the guard said.

Mary was unperturbed. She was used to this kind of nonsense. "Then, give him my compliments, and tell him I will call upon him." And with that, Mary Walker went on her way.

Who was this rebel—a woman so radical that even leaders of the women's suffrage movement (the fight for a woman's right to vote) found her "very queer"? Was she really so odd, or queer, as people outside the mainstream were called at the time? More likely, she was one hundred years ahead of her time. She demanded the kind of respect and power that had been reserved for men. While that status eluded her for much of her life, she became a celebrity of her time and paved the way for future generations of women.

CHAPTER 1

THE MAKING OF A REBEL

MARY EDWARDS WALKER ENTERED THE WORLD on November 26, 1832, fifty-six years after her great-grandfather fought in the Revolutionary War (1775–1783), the fight for American independence from Great Britain. Like her great-grandfather, Mary would become a true revolutionary, one who declared her own independence from conventional thought.

Her parents, Vesta and Alvah Walker, along with their four daughters, had recently moved from Syracuse, New York, to a farm just outside of Oswego, a thriving village 40 miles (64 km) north on the eastern shore of Lake Ontario. They were in the heart of New York's Finger Lakes region, a place of uncommon natural beauty. The Finger Lakes, so named because they are shaped like long, thin fingers, were originally home to six Indigenous nations: the Mohawk, Oneida, Onondaga, Cayuga, Seneca, and Tuscarora. Between 1570 and 1600, the nations established a sophisticated political and social alliance that may be one of the oldest examples of formal democracy. The resulting Iroquois Confederacy, or Haudenosaunee, created a constitution called the Great Law of Peace, which declares a respect for the rights of all people. Each nation selects representatives to serve on the Grand Council; when laws are made, all council members must agree on the issue. Women are an integral part of the decision-making process. The Founding Fathers of the United States, including Benjamin Franklin, were familiar with the Great Law of Peace, and it is believed to be a model for the US Constitution.

Later, a sizable number of Quakers—members of the Religious Society of Friends—settled in the region, and their pacifist (opposing war and violence) beliefs and opposition to slavery attracted other like-minded people, including American writer Mark Twain, who spent twenty summers on a farm belonging to his sister-in-law just outside the town of Elmira.

The Walker farm was located in Oswego Town on Bunker Hill Road. The village was situated along the Oswego River on the northern border of Oswego County. Syracuse, New York, is located along the southern border of the county.

This is where he wrote much of *The Adventures of Tom Sawyer* and *Adventures of Huckleberry Finn*. In the mid-nineteenth century, a group of men and women in Oneida formed a community called the Perfectionists. They believed that men and women were equal, that free love (the freedom to marry, divorce, and bear children without social restriction or government interference) should be encouraged, and that the entire community was responsible for raising children. Many leaders of the women's suffrage movement—including Elizabeth Cady Stanton and Susan B. Anthony—called the Finger Lakes region home.

Alvah Walker built a white frame house on Bunker Hill Road, where Mary was born. Alvah loved astronomy, and he and Vesta had named their older daughters with an eye to the heavens. Like her mother, the oldest girl was named Vesta, which is also the name of a large asteroid. The second, Aurora Borealis, was named after the spectacular northern lights. Luna's name was derived from the Latin word for "moon," and the name of the fourth daughter, Cynthia, was the Latin name of the Greek moon goddess. The Walkers' firstborn child, a son named Abel, had died shortly after his birth.

Vesta and Alvah broke their naming pattern when their fifth daughter was born. They named her Mary Edwards, after an aunt on the Walker side of the family. A year later, her little brother, Alvah Jr., was born. Mary, with her ordinary name, found her own way to make her mark, even though, as she later wrote, "I was naturally timid as a girl, but had to overcome this through strong convictions of duty and I have felt that I must do what I believed was right regardless of consequences. I do not deserve credit for standing up to my principles for I could not do otherwise."

★ ★ ★

The farm on Bunker Hill Road was fertile ground for the seeds of the progressive ideas that Mary would later champion, such as equal rights for women and people of color. Vesta and Alvah wanted to make sure that their daughters received a quality education—which was rarely given to girls in the 1830s. With the help of their neighbors, they built a schoolhouse on their property. Alvah and Vesta, and later their older daughters, became the school's first teachers. Although Alvah's formal schooling had ended when he was thirteen, after the death of his father, he loved to read. When he was a young man, he contracted the measles, which in turn caused him breathing problems. Much of his recovery was spent reading all the medical books he could get his hands on. He gained enough knowledge to provide some basic medical care to his family and neighbors—and collected a great library of medical texts that the teenage Mary would devour.

Even simpler housedresses such as this one sported wide skirts and formfitting bodices in the 1830s. These heavy skirts and tight corsets made working on a farm difficult.

Alvah's medical studies led him to the conclusion that the tight-fitting corsets worn by women at the time were damaging their health by putting pressure on their internal organs and making it difficult to breathe. Vesta and the girls all helped work on the farm. Planting and harvesting crops just wasn't compatible with constricting corsets, fluffy petticoats, and wide hoopskirts. Alvah advised his daughters and wife to wear loose-fitting dresses that allowed freedom of movement, and Mary embraced his advice wholeheartedly.

While Alvah and Vesta raised their children to believe in a higher power, they were freethinkers. They encouraged Mary and her siblings to ask questions about religion. Mary became interested in a new religious movement called spiritualism, which taught that the spirits of the dead could communicate with

Sisters Kate (*left*) and Maggie Fox (*right*) created an elaborate hoax that sparked a fascination with spiritualism.

I Could Not Do Otherwise

the living. The movement began in the United States with Kate and Maggie Fox, eleven- and fourteen-year-old sisters living in a small town near Rochester, New York. In 1848 the girls said they had communicated with the spirit of a peddler murdered in their house five years earlier. (One of the girls later admitted that the spiritual communications were actually an elaborate hoax.) Many advocates of women's rights embraced spiritualism. Unlike mainstream religions, it was one of the first religious movements in the United States that encouraged women to speak before audiences of both men and women. And spiritualists were staunch abolitionists and supported the end of slavery—a movement that was highly important to the Walker family.

The antislavery movement was so important to Vesta and Alvah Walker that their home in Oswego Town became a stop on the Underground Railroad, the network of safe houses and hideouts that helped Black people escape slavery in the South. In 1849 antislavery crusader Frederick Douglass, a former enslaved person, gave a lecture in their town. Historians don't know whether sixteen-year-old Mary attended the event or met Douglass, but it seems likely that the Walker family would have wanted to be there. Years later, Mary and Douglass would become well acquainted through their common activism in the women's rights and abolition movements.

Just a year earlier, in 1848, Elizabeth Cady Stanton and Lucretia Mott had organized the nation's first women's rights convention, held in nearby Seneca Falls. There, speakers called for moral, economic, and political equality for women. Again, historians don't know whether Mary attended the convention, which helped launch the women's suffrage movement, but she and her family certainly would have known about it and wholeheartedly supported it.

ALL MEN AND WOMEN ARE CREATED EQUAL
The Seneca Falls Convention

Elizabeth Cady Stanton and Lucretia Mott met at the 1840 World Anti-Slavery Convention in London, which they attended with their husbands. Stanton, a women's rights advocate, and Mott, a Quaker preacher, were barred from the convention floor because of their gender. They were incensed and resolved to do something about it. With the aid of a handful of other women, they organized the Seneca Falls Convention, the first-ever women's rights convention in the United States, held on July 19–20, 1848, in Seneca Falls, New York.

Despite scant publicity about the event, three hundred people—most of them locals—showed up for the convention. On the first day, which was open to women only, Stanton read her Declaration of Sentiments. This document, which was modeled

Elizabeth Cady Stanton (*left*) and Lucretia Mott (*right*) are two of the most widely recognized leaders of the women's suffrage movement in the United States. Mott was twenty years older than Stanton and served as a mentor to the younger woman.

closely on the US Declaration of Independence, called upon women to organize and petition for the same rights and freedoms that were granted to men. It began,

> **When, in the course of human events, it becomes necessary for one portion of the family of man to assume among the people of the earth a position different from that which they have hitherto occupied, but one to which the laws of nature and of nature's God entitle them, a decent respect to the opinions of mankind requires that they should declare the causes that impel them to such a course.**
>
> **We hold these truths to be self-evident: that all men and women are created equal; that they are endowed by their Creator with certain inalienable rights.**

Men were invited to the second day of the convention, and perhaps none had more influence on the outcome of the event than Frederick Douglass, who was the only Black man there. The conference attendants discussed eleven resolutions about women's rights. They called upon American citizens to regard any laws that treated women as less than equal to men as having "no force or authority." All the resolutions passed unanimously except for the ninth, which called for women "to secure to themselves their sacred right to the elective franchise"—that is, the right to vote. The resolution was highly controversial; many thought that women had no place in politics.

Even Lucretia Mott and her husband opposed the resolution, which Stanton had written. "Why Lizzie, thee will make us look ridiculous," she told her friend.

Douglass backed Stanton's resolution with a passionate defense, saying that denying women the right to participate in government was not just a great injustice, but that it deprived the government of "one half of the moral and intellectual power . . . of the world." The resolution passed, but as some in the women's rights movement predicted, it provoked a great deal of ridicule and scorn.

A typical response appeared in the *Oneida (Utica, NY) Whig*, a newspaper from nearby Utica: "This bolt is the most shocking and unnatural incident ever recorded in the history of womanity. If our ladies will insist on voting and legislating, where, gentleman, will be our dinners and our elbows? Where our domestic firesides and the holes in our stockings?" The implication was that women who vote would somehow be less inclined to take care of household chores such as cooking and mending.

Mary, more than any of her siblings, took her parents' progressive ideas and ran with them. When Mary was a teenager, an article in a newspaper caught her eye. An American Christian missionary (religious worker) in India said there was a need for female doctors who could help care for Indian women. Mary was intrigued and decided she wanted to become a missionary doctor. She immersed herself in her father's medical texts, reading about the human body and hygiene. Hygiene was a trending topic in the mid-nineteenth century. People were beginning to learn that germs, which thrived on unwashed hands and bodies, could both cause disease and transmit it from person to person. Social reformers like the Walkers embraced the idea that cleanliness was essential to public health—a notion that was not widely accepted by the medical establishment at that time. Doctors often didn't wash their hands between caring for patients. They used dirty rags to wrap wounds. Because of this, and because no one yet knew about medicines such as antibiotics, many people died of infectious diseases.

One of Mary's favorite writers was Dr. Calvin Cutter, who was also an active and outspoken abolitionist. A doctor who wanted to better the world inspired the idealistic Mary.

Mary soon dropped the idea of becoming a missionary doctor; maybe she realized that her unconventional ideas about spirituality might not be a good fit for the life of a Christian missionary. When in 1848 sixteen-year-old Mary told her parents about her desire to become a doctor, they wholeheartedly supported her—which is remarkable considering that there were no women doctors at the time. To be sure, women had been successful midwives and healers for centuries, assisting women in childbirth and treating patients with traditional medicines, but most mainstream medical schools refused to admit women. In the eyes of nineteenth-century men, a woman's place was in the home if she was married. (If she was single, teaching was an acceptable profession.) An 1848 medical text stated that "she [a woman] has a head almost too small for the intellect but just large enough for love."

One medical journal railed against a school in Ohio for awarding a medical degree to a woman in 1859, writing, "There never was a woman fitted to practice medicine, surgery, and obstetrics [the branch of medicine dealing with birth], no matter how long she may have studied."

This was the kind of toxic attitude that women wishing to enter male-dominated fields had to endure then. Elizabeth Blackwell broke the gender barrier in medicine in 1849 when she graduated first in her class from the Geneva Medical College in upstate New York. She became the first female doctor in America. Mary was surely inspired by Blackwell's example.

Mary continued her studies at a nearby women's preparatory school, Falley Seminary in Fulton, New York. She studied at Falley for one year, taking courses in algebra, natural philosophy (science), grammar, physiology, and hygiene. Eager to move forward with her plans,

Elizabeth Blackwell was the first woman to receive a medical degree in the United States. She eventually opened her own medical college in 1868 to train more female physicians.

Mary left Falley when she was nineteen to begin teaching at a school in Minetto, New York. She hadn't abandoned her plans to become a doctor—not at all. She needed to pay her way through medical school, and her family didn't have enough money to help. It was up to her to earn her school tuition.

Mary began to experiment with her clothing during her teaching years. She had never worn a corset, later telling an interviewer, "No, sir; my waist has never been confined in one of those steel traps; it is just as nature intended it should be—free and unconfined." Now she took things further. She shortened her loose-waisted skirts to mid-calf and added pants underneath, because at this time, a woman could not expose a bare leg, not even an ankle. She later raised her skirts to just above the knee, causing a great deal of tut-tutting among the locals—and more.

"I have endured all sorts of obstacles to overcome," she told the interviewer. "One afternoon I was walking along a country road when a farmer started a mob of small boys after me. They threw stones and foul eggs and anything they could lay their hands on. But I finally escaped from them without being seriously hurt." Mary, who stood just over 5 feet (1.5 m) tall and weighed less than 100 pounds (45 kg), took the abuse in stride. She proudly added that the farmer became one of her best friends after she successfully treated him for a serious illness that had caused other doctors in the county to throw up their hands in confusion. She said, "I succeeded in bringing him about all right."

After teaching for nearly two years, Mary had saved enough money for medical school. She would attend school for three thirteen-week terms.

Just after her twenty-first birthday, in December 1853, she was accepted into Syracuse Medical College, one of the few medical schools that admitted women. Syracuse taught a type of medicine known as eclecticism, as opposed to the conventional medicine of this era. Conventional medical doctors used some fairly brutal treatments at that time, including blood-letting (draining large amounts of blood by cutting a vein was thought to let poisons out of the body) and harsh drugs containing mercury (itself a poison). Eclectic doctors favored a variety of gentler remedies, including herbal medicines. In general, conventional doctors thought eclectic doctors were quacks, and eclectic doctors thought conventional doctors had no interest in scientific investigation into new practices.

Mary studied the usual medical school subjects, including anatomy, physiology, surgery, obstetrics, and chemistry. But the eclectic medical college also offered courses in diet and hygiene, two topics that Mary was particularly interested in. She studied new treatments, including hydropathy—sometimes called the water cure. Hydropathy was based on the idea that people could purge their bodies of impurities through treatment with wet bandages, steam rooms, hot and cold baths, and drinking lots of water.

On February 20, 1855, Syracuse Medical College awarded Mary a doctor of medicine degree with honors. She was one of three graduating students asked to deliver a speech at the awards ceremony. In it, she spoke ardently on behalf of all women who wished to drink "of the clear waters of the fountain of science. . . . Let me pursue the studies for which I have the greatest taste—theology, law, medicine, or whatever it may be."

Mary's address contained hints of what would drive her actions for the rest of her life: a desire for

The water cure took many forms. This illustration highlights six different hydrotherapies such as wearing layers of clothes to encourage sweating and taking various types of baths.

greatness—and fame. "May you . . . long write your names on the highest tablet of fame," she told her fellow students. "May it be said of some that they have risen to eminence as medical authors, as teachers, or as college founders—and of *all* that they are renowned for goodness."

One of the other speakers at the graduation ceremony was Mary's friend Albert Miller. He spoke of the value of eclectic medical colleges. We are living, he said, in "an age of progress." The person who represents "the greatest individual of the age . . . is the *liberal* thinker," because that person is "free from all prejudice" and breathes the "vivifying atmosphere of science." He concluded, "Oh! *success to eclecticism, the God-send of the medical mind.*"

Mary had originally hoped to treat soldiers fighting in the Crimean War after graduation. British, French, and Turkish armies had been at war with Russian forces, mainly on the Crimean Peninsula in modern-day Ukraine, since 1853. American newspapers reported on horrific, unsanitary conditions in British military hospitals there, where more soldiers died of diseases such as typhus, typhoid fever, dysentery, and cholera than from battle wounds. She may have been inspired by the famous British nurse Florence Nightingale, who worked tirelessly to care for the soldiers in that war and to clean up filthy hospital wards.

The Crimean War was winding down by the time Mary received her degree, so she settled for a much less adventurous destination: Columbus, Ohio, where her father's sister lived. With a recommendation from a male doctor in Cincinnati, she hoped to set up a private practice. But, like many early female physicians, she struggled to make a living. Many people just weren't ready to accept a female doctor. Meanwhile, she and

Albert had been corresponding, and what had been a friendship blossomed into love. She soon moved to Rome, New York, where Albert had set up his own private practice.

Mary and Albert were married on November 16, 1855, in the Walker family home. She was not quite twenty-three years old. Their wedding was as unconventional as Mary and Albert themselves. She wore a shortened skirt over pants. During the ceremony, the minister, a member of the liberal Unitarian Church and staunch advocate of women's rights, did not ask Mary to vow to obey her husband, as was normally done at that time. "The noble Rev. Mr. May would not stoop to such a despicable meanness as to ask a woman to 'serve' or 'obey' a man," Mary later said. "How barbarous the very idea of one equal promising to be the slave of another, instead of both entering life's greatest drama as intelligent equal parties. Our promises were such as denotes, two intelligent beings instead of one intelligent and one chained."

Mary also insisted on keeping her last name, although she sometimes signed her name "Miller-Walker." When she and Albert set up a joint practice, the sign over the entrance to their clinic read "Miller and Walker, Physicians." They had separate offices, each with their own clientele. It was to be, Mary hoped, a professional partnership and a marriage based on mutual love and commitment to social reform.

CHAPTER 2

A CHAMPION OF WOMEN'S CAUSES

MARY SPENT THOSE FIRST FEW YEARS in Rome building her medical practice, driving her own horse and carriage to make house calls. She initially thought she would limit her clients to women and children, but some female patients found her such a good doctor that they asked her to treat their husbands as well. One of her patients, Harriet Harris, became a "beloved friend." Harris later wrote that she had long suffered from chronic pain but that "Dr. Walker has positively cured me."

Mary's growing practice kept her busy, but treating children for croup and setting broken bones did little to challenge her restless mind. She found purpose in a new cause that would define her for the rest of her life: dress reform. By this time, she had been experimenting with different outfits, all including pants. "I had ten or twelve different suits with the skirts of different lengths and the trousers reaching to my shoes," Mary told an interviewer. "No matter what length skirt I wore somebody considered it his or her Christian duty to tell me that I ought to wear some other length."

À LA BLOOMER

In the nineteenth century, middle- and upper-class women commonly wore as many as eight petticoats, which together could weigh as much as 10 pounds (4.5 kg); tight corsets; bustles that stuck out in back and tied around the waist; and dresses with long skirts that dragged on the ground. A few women cross-dressed, passing as men to work as cowboys or soldiers, and working-class women wore practical clothing such as simple shifts as a matter of necessity. But it was rare for middle- or upper-class women to wear pants in public.

In 1851 Elizabeth Smith Miller, the daughter of a prominent antislavery activist in New York, was sick of working in her garden wearing petticoats and a corset. She resolved that "this shackle should no longer be endured." She began wearing loose-fitting pants that tapered to a tight fit around the ankles—so-called Turkish trousers, modeled after traditional pants worn by Turkish men and women—and a skirt that fell a few inches below the knee.

Delighted with her new outfit, Miller wore it to visit her cousin Elizabeth Cady Stanton in Seneca Falls. Stanton introduced Miller to

Teacher and political activist Amelia Jenks Bloomer was very active in the community in Seneca Falls. This illustration from 1851 shows Bloomer in her freedom costume.

her friend and neighbor Amelia Jenks Bloomer. Soon the three of them were strolling through the streets of Seneca Falls wearing shortened skirts and Turkish trousers, much to the shock of their neighbors. Bloomer wrote articles about their new outfits, with illustrations and instructions on how to sew them, for a women's rights magazine she had founded two years earlier. National papers picked up the story, and soon the unusual outfit was called the "Bloomer costume," although women who wore it preferred "freedom costume."

The idea of women wearing pants captured the public's imagination, and songs such as "The Bloomer's Complaint" became popular:

> **Dear me, what a terrible clatter they raise**
> **Because that old gossip Dame Rumor**
> **Declares, with her hands lifted up in amaze**
> **That I'm coming out as a Bloomer,**
> **That I'm coming out as a Bloomer.**
> **I wonder how often these men must be told**
> **When a woman a notion once seizes,**
> **However they ridicule, lecture or scold,**
> **She'll do, after all, as she pleases,**
> **She'll do, after all, as she pleases.**

But not everyone was so enthusiastic. In fact, most public reaction was swift and brutal. Opponents to dress reform feared that women who wore pants would become more like men. In November 1851, the *International Monthly* wrote that women who wore the freedom dress were "ridiculous and indecent . . . an abandoned class . . . vulgar women whose inordinate love of notoriety is apt to display itself in ways that induce their exclusion from respectable society."

Stanton feared that the backlash would hurt the cause of women's suffrage, and eventually all three women gave up on the costume. "We put the dress on for greater freedom," Stanton told a fellow suffragist, "but what is physical freedom compared with mental bondage?"

Miller, under pressure from her father, "found myself again in the bonds of the old swaddling (restrictive) clothes—a victim to my love of beauty." And Bloomer, the last holdout of the three, gave up the freedom dress for practical reasons.

She and her husband had moved to windy Council Bluffs, Iowa, and she was "greatly annoyed and mortified" when high winds blew her shortened skirt up over her head. She tried loading the hem of the skirt with buckshot, only to end up with bruised legs when wind whipped the skirt around her legs. She, too, abandoned her namesake Bloomer costume.

To Mary, dress reform was about more than just wearing comfortable clothing. As a doctor, she believed that the new style of dress was healthier. "The snug fit of the waist of the Dress or corsets," she wrote, "prevents freedom of motion, of respiration, digestion . . . circulation of the blood. . . . It prevents the freedom of the muscles of the lower part of the chest, and the upper part of the leg; producing a weariness of the bony structure, both at their origin and insertion." She argued that long skirts were a health hazard not just because they were heavy but also because they dragged on the ground, picking up all sorts of filth. Additionally, women had to worry about tripping over their long skirts while carrying babies or burning candles.

Having liberated herself from cumbersome and constrictive clothing, Mary made it her goal to encourage other women to do the same—and to make her more practical style of dress acceptable to society. She found an outlet for her ideas in a new publication called the *Sibyl: A Review of the Tastes, Errors, and Fashions of Society*. In ancient Greek myths, a sibyl was a female prophet said to have a direct line of communication with the gods. The founders of the *Sibyl*, Dr. Lydia Sayer Hasbrouck and her newlywed husband, John Hasbrouck, hoped that their paper would not just predict but shape the future of women in society.

Like Mary, Sayer Hasbrouck studied hydropathy, and the two women bonded over their shared passion for medicine, dress reform, and women's equality. Mary's letters and articles

This issue of the *Sibyl* from September 1, 1856, features an illustration of a woman wearing a reform dress. The newspaper frequently included articles about dress reform and the water cure as well as popular news stories.

in the *Sibyl* addressed not just dress reform but women's rights in general.

In April 1859, she weighed in on one of the most sensational murder cases of the time. On February 27, 1859, US congressman Daniel Sickles had shot and killed Philip Barton Key (the son of Francis Scott Key, who wrote the "Star-Spangled Banner") across the street from the White House. Sickles suspected that his wife was having an affair with Key, who was the district attorney for the District of Columbia (DC) and had a reputation as a ladies' man.

The press covered the event in all its scandalous detail. They depicted Sickles as a well-respected man who was wronged by his wife. She, on the other hand, was portrayed as a "fallen woman" who was guiltier than Key in their affair because she

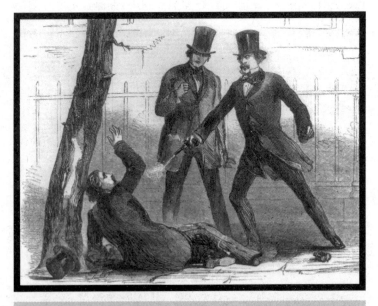

Illustrations of Daniel Sickles and Philip Barton Key's altercation such as this one often depicted Sickles standing over Key. This illustration was printed in *Harper's Weekly*.

had led him along. Sickles's attorney argued that his client was not responsible for his actions because the affair had driven him insane. On April 26 of that year, a jury found Sickles not guilty by reason of insanity—the first successful insanity defense in the US court system.

What didn't come out in the trial was that Sickles was himself a rake. Before he married sixteen-year-old Teresa Bagioli in 1852, he had been in a relationship with Fanny White, a prostitute and later a madam of a brothel in New York City. He had paraded her around in front of his friends and colleagues. After his marriage, he continued to see White and even took her to England on a diplomatic trip, where she was introduced to Queen Victoria. Teresa Sickles, meanwhile, was at home pregnant.

Mary was outraged at the double standard applied to Teresa Sickles. In a front-page article in the May 15, 1859, issue of the *Sibyl*, she wrote that Teresa Sickles should not be held more responsible for the affair than Key because "never, until women as a mass are better educated physiologically [regarding health]—until they are considered something besides a drudge or a doll—until they have all the social education and political advantages the men enjoy; in a word, *equality* with them, shall we consider vice in our sex any more culpable than in men." She signed her article, "Yours in charity for our own sex, Dr. Walker."

Later that year, she wrote multiple articles urging readers of the *Sibyl* to support the construction of a state-run foundling hospital—a home to care for unwed mothers and their children. At the time, birth control was unreliable and was also not something a "respectable" woman used. Women who became pregnant outside of marriage had two options: give birth to children they could probably not afford to raise and face a lifetime of disgrace or obtain an illegal and probably unsafe abortion. In the 1850s, abortion was illegal in New York State except to save the life of the mother. Mary believed that a foundling hospital would encourage unmarried mothers to entrust their children to the care of others and give the mothers a second chance in life.

In the August 1, 1859, issue of the *Sibyl*, she urged compassion for unwed mothers: "Shall a woman's few sins merit everlasting condemnation? Does she not deserve one kind word or look? Has she forfeited all claim to being recognized as a human being? Do you expect that kicking her down the hill will in time transform her into an angel with wings to fly to the top again?" This article she signed, "Yours in every woman's cause, Mary E. Miller Walker, MD."

The foundling hospital never came to be, in part due to a lack of support from the state, as well as the looming Civil War between the northern and southern states over slavery, state's rights, and westward expansion. In October 1859, abolitionist John Brown led a raid on a federal armory in Harpers Ferry, Virginia, in an attempt to start an armed revolt of enslaved people that would bring an end to slavery. Although the raid failed and Brown was hanged for treason and murder in December, it was clear that the nation was on the brink of splitting in two over the issue of slavery.

Mary, perhaps anticipating the coming conflict, wrote an article for the *Sibyl* titled "Women Soldiers." She rejected an idea put forth by many conservatives: that women should not have the right to vote because they did not fight in wars. She pointed out that women such as Margaret Corbin, a nurse who took over her husband's position at the cannon after he was killed, had fought in the Revolutionary War to help men gain the rights they—but not women—enjoyed. She informed "Mr. or Miss Conservative" that, should war break out, many women who wore bloomers would be proud to serve in the military. Mary believed that women who were brave enough to wear the dress reform costume were more than ready to become soldiers—and to participate fully in politics.

It was around this time that Mary joined the lecture circuit, speaking about women's rights, dress reform, and abolition. In a time before television and the movies, public lectures were a form of both entertainment and information. Mary delivered. She urged her mostly female audiences to "throw away their embroidery and read Mental Philosophy, Moral Science and Physiology" and to throw off their "dressical" chains "so they more go forth free, sensible women." Not only were the lectures a way to spread the word about her passions, but they were also an additional source of income, paid for by sponsors.

As far as the public knew, things were going well for Mary. Her medical practice was taking off, and she was establishing a respected name for herself as an advocate of women's rights and other social causes. But her private life was falling apart. Earlier in 1859, she discovered that Albert had been having an affair with at least one woman. She was hurt and furious and demanded a divorce. Albert shrugged it off. Why not, he suggested, claim "the same *privileges*" as a man and find a lover of her own?

She told her brother-in-law L. J. Worden, who was boarding with them and witnessed their fight, that she "would never live with a man who was so *vile* as to make such a proposition to a *wife*, and that people who thought her so *happy* knew little of her *wretchedness*."

Mary may have had progressive ideas, but they did not include having an open marriage. She kicked Albert out of the house and by the spring of 1860 had relocated her medical office to another location in town.

It was difficult to obtain a divorce in the state of New York at that time. She had to prove that Albert was cheating on her, which wouldn't be easy—and was likely to stir up a lot of gossip. What's more, there was a five-year waiting period between the time a divorce was granted and when it became final. Mary was not known for her patience, so she searched for other options.

Mary learned that the state of Iowa had much more liberal divorce laws, with one catch: she had to live in the state for six months before filing for divorce. To meet this requirement, she moved in with family friends, Albert Emerson and Louisa House in Delhi, Iowa, in 1860.

Mary didn't have a license to legally practice medicine in the state of Iowa, but she wasn't about to sit back and twiddle her thumbs while she waited to file for divorce. She had been studying German on her own and was determined to use her downtime to become more fluent. In the fall of 1860, she enrolled in the Bowen Collegiate Institute in Hopkinton, about 8 miles (13 km) south of Delhi. After she paid her tuition, Mary learned that the school was not teaching German that semester—even though it had been listed among the school's offerings.

Mary was tired of broken promises. She threatened to sue the cash-strapped college if it did not come through with a German class. That was the whole reason she had enrolled at Bowen!

While Mary waited to see whether Bowen would provide the promised German class, she decided to attend an evening

Bowen Collegiate Institute opened in 1858, only two years before Mary enrolled. The original school building pictured here easily accommodated the first graduating class, though the school expanded after the Civil War.

meeting of a debate club organized by some male students at Bowen. She thought debate might help her develop skills in public lecturing. At the end of the evening, she asked if she could become a member of the all-male society. After a vote, the men welcomed Mary into their club and invited her to take part in the next week's debate.

But Bowen's director of women students found out about her plans. She declared that Mary was absolutely forbidden to take part in such an unladylike activity! Mary ignored her order. The society was a town organization, not a school club, so the school should have no say in her participation, she argued. Mary believed that what she did on her own time was nobody's business but her own. She attended the meeting and was promptly suspended from Bowen. The male students in the debate society joined Mary in a protest march through the town, with Mary in the lead. Those men were also suspended, and although they were later allowed to return to Bowen, Mary was not.

Meanwhile, Mary learned that New York would not recognize out-of-state divorces. Having been expelled from Bowen and unable to practice medicine in Iowa, she moved back to Rome, New York, where she reopened her medical practice and hired a divorce attorney. A private investigator found that Albert had had several affairs during their six-year marriage and had fathered at least one child. Finally, in September 1861, Mary was granted her divorce. Following New York State law, she would have to wait five more years for the divorce to be final. After that, she would be free to remarry if she wanted.

CHAPTER 3

CIVIL WAR SURGEON

MARY'S PERSONAL MISFORTUNES PLAYED OUT against the backdrop of a much more serious national tragedy: civil war. Abraham Lincoln was elected the sixteenth president of the United States on November 6, 1860. A member of the Republican Party, Lincoln vowed to prohibit the expansion of slavery into the nation's western territories. Citizens in southern states, economically dependent on the labor of enslaved people feared that his election signaled the end of their ability to determine the course of national politics. The governments of South Carolina, Mississippi, Florida, Alabama, Georgia, Louisiana, Texas, Virginia, Arkansas, Tennessee, and North Carolina declared their intention to secede (withdraw) from the Union during the winter of 1860–1861 and formed the Confederate States of America.

War officially broke out on April 12, 1861, when Confederate forces opened fire on the federal government's garrison at Fort Sumter, South Carolina. Union forces surrendered the battle for the garrison thirty-four hours later.

Mary followed the developments in the war from her home in New York. Like many women, Mary was eager to help in any way she could. Shortly after the war began in April, the author of *Little Women*, Louisa May Alcott, wrote in her diary, "I long to be a man; but as I can't fight, I will content myself with working for those who can."

Some women *did* disguise themselves as men and fight in the war, but many more collected supplies for the soldiers: food, clothing, bedding, and medical items. Dorothea Dix, who had made a name for herself by advocating for the mentally ill, helped recruit women nurses for the Union. Most of these women were unpaid volunteers, since the Union barely had enough money to pay its soldiers.

Mary wanted to aid Union soldiers, but she was also motivated by the plight of enslaved women. She believed "the interests of the cruelly-abused coloured women had the strongest claim" on her war efforts, and she "was confident that the God of justice would not allow the war to end without [the emancipation of enslaved people]."

Dorothea Dix toured hospitals for the mentally ill and reported their treatments and conditions to the public and politicians. She helped establish new hospitals in several states before the start of the Civil War.

Mary decided she could best help the war effort by volunteering her services as a physician. She discussed the idea with her family, who supported her—especially her father, Alvah. Following the bloody Battle of Bull Run in Manassas, Virginia, in late July, Washington, DC, was overwhelmed with sick and wounded soldiers. Hospitals were overflowing. Churches, private homes, the unfinished Patent Office Building, and even tents in vacant lots were turned into makeshift hospitals. They were in dire need of physicians. So, soon after her divorce was granted in September, she boarded a train headed to the nation's capital. Mary wasted no time once she arrived in October 1861. She headed straight to the War Department at Seventeenth Street and Pennsylvania Avenue and asked to see the secretary of war, Simon Cameron. This may seem awfully brash, even for Mary, but things were different back then. Ordinary citizens could arrange meetings with government officials, even the president. Mary asked to be appointed an acting assistant surgeon, which carried with it the rank and pay of an army lieutenant.

Cameron refused, telling her that the US military did not allow female officers, nor did the army hire women doctors. Cameron had appointed Dorothea Dix superintendent of army nurses just a few months earlier. But Dix held no rank in the army, and her job, caring for sick and injured soldiers under the supervision of male doctors, was considered acceptable work for a woman.

Never one to let gender discrimination get in her way, Mary went to one of the largest hospitals in Washington, DC, at the time, Indiana Hospital, in the unfinished Patent Office Building. She asked the surgeon in charge of the hospital, Dr. J. N. Green, if she might work as his assistant surgeon. She knew that he was the only medical officer in a hospital with eighty to one hundred patients and that he must be in dire need of an assistant. He agreed but warned her that the physician working there before her had died of overwork. Mary wasn't dissuaded.

Green wrote a letter to Surgeon General Clement A. Finley, asking that she receive a commission (appointment) as his

Though construction was not completed until 1868, the Patent Office Building's large open halls offered enough space to house many injured and ill soldiers during the Civil War.

assistant. He said she was well qualified and came with the highest of recommendations.

Finley turned him down: he "could not appoint a woman." Mary turned to Assistant Surgeon General Robert C. Wood, who had no objections but didn't want to go over the head of Finley, his boss.

So Mary decided to volunteer her services without pay while she continued her efforts to get a commission. She told Green she "would be his assistant surgeon just the same as though I had been appointed."

Mary worked at the Indiana Hospital until the end of the year. She wrote to her family in Oswego Town that she was an assistant to Green and worked with "five very nice lady nurses and a number of gentleman nurses," adding that "every soul in the Hospital has to abide by my orders as much as though Dr. Green had given them."

One evening Mary left the hospital to take a walk. As she passed in front of the Treasury Building, a "dude," as she called him, asked how far she was going. Mary felt threatened. She drew a revolver and pointed it at the young man, saying that she could kill six just like him. The man made a hasty retreat, looking back at every step. This amused Mary, who fired a bullet into the ground when she thought no one was watching. A police officer who heard the shot came to investigate. "I fired the ball for the purpose of giving those dudes to understand upon what ground I stood," she told a journalist, "believing that those of his class who believe that there are no women capable of taking care of themselves when young, would inform their friends that they might be in danger of their lives if they approached me."

While working at Indiana Hospital, Mary lived in the Patent Office Building, both to save money and to be on call overnight whenever a doctor was needed, giving Green a much-needed break. She later wrote that her assistance "no doubt prevented him also from passing away from overwork as did his predecessor." One of her duties was to screen incoming patients for symptoms of smallpox. Mary had received the smallpox vaccine—a preparatory injection that builds up the body's defenses to a disease—and was protected from getting sick, but many soldiers were not. The deadly disease had spread quickly through the army camps. She sent infected soldiers to a separate hospital specifically set up to treat them without allowing the disease to spread further.

Mary became a favorite of the soldiers in Indiana Hospital. Not only was she a good doctor, but she also took the time to talk with the soldiers and write letters for them. Once, she was walking through the wards when the mood seemed particularly gloomy, so she made a point to greet every patient with a smile and some kind words. She later wrote in her journal,

> *I took up a photograph case that was on a stand by one very young soldier and said in quite a pleasant manner, "I suppose the sweetest face in the world is in that case." He said, "Yes, you open it and you will see the sweetest face that I ever saw." I opened it expecting, of course, to see the face of some girl that he thought more of than any one in the world who lived in his section of the country, and opening it I found it was a looking glass. What little circumstance no doubt cheered that soldier many a time as he thought of my surprised face.*

No doubt it cheered Mary too.

Mary's reputation as a kind and caring doctor spread to the soldiers' families. A woman from New Jersey, Elizabeth Conklin, wrote to Mary on behalf of her husband. He had been arrested on charges of desertion (leaving the army without permission) but had written to tell his wife that he had been released from military custody and should be home within a week. Two weeks had passed and still Conklin had not seen her husband. She begged Mary for some news—any news—about her husband. "I am so much in need of his help," she wrote. "I feel pretty well at present but my babes is all the time sick." The outcome of this story is lost to history, but Conklin's letter pleading for help was one of many that Mary received during her time at the hospital, and she put a great deal of effort into helping everyone who asked.

PLEAS FOR HELP

With casualties (killed and wounded soldiers) mounting in early 1863, Congress passed the Enrollment Act, which required states in the North that had not enlisted enough volunteer soldiers to draft men into the army. But wealthy men had an out. They could either pay $300 (the equivalent of about $6,500 in twenty-first-century money) to skip the draft or could hire a substitute to take their place in the army. This system led critics to call the Civil War a "rich man's war and a poor man's fight." Most men were too poor to buy their way out of the army. One of them wrote to Mary:

> I am a drafted man and am in a bad condition and I cannot get any satisfaction from my Doctors. I was sick when I was drafted & was not able to do a days work. . . . I being a poor man i could not get a substitute therefore I was oblige to come myself. . . . When I was a small boy I fell from a tree and ever since that time my left shoulder has been verry weak . . . but it makes no difference hear where I am now for they compell me to shoulder my knapsack and march with the Regt. . . . I never was helthy nor verry strong my constitution is weak and feeble now if you can render my any assistence do it as soon as you can possably can. . . . There is going to be an examination in a few days and if I have a letter from you it may help me.

Thomas Kelly, writing to Mary on behalf of himself and two other soldiers, who were probably illiterate, wrote,

Madam Walker

I now write you a few lines to let you know that am far away from home a prisoner they hold me and two other men their names is (Joseph Brynner Nicholas Callaway.) I and these two men are arrested as Deserters belonging to the Eighteenth Reg. Marm we have never seen that regiment before they sent (us) to it I am a sailor by trade and have lost my father and four brothers in this war and you will be rewarded some future day I never was a soldier yet but I want you to come up and see me anser soon Your Obident servant,

Signed as follows

Thomas Kelly
Joseph Brynner (x mark)
Nicholas Callaway (x mark)

    It's not clear whether Mary was able to help the men who wrote these letters, but we know that she did something remarkable: she represented an accused deserter in court in 1863—and won his freedom, back pay from the army, and a thirty-day leave to visit his family back home. The presiding judge, Colonel Alexander, noted that this was "the first time a woman had acted as an attorney" in this type of case in the capital.

One of Mary's biggest challenges at Indiana Hospital was practicing her brand of eclectic medicine in a hospital that placed its faith in conventional medicine. Mary found herself at odds with new surgeons who came to join Dr. Green's staff, especially regarding how to handle amputations. It was common during the Civil War for surgeons to amputate an injured arm or leg. Doctors believed that if they removed a wounded limb quickly, before infection set in, they had a better chance of saving the patient's life. The problem was that amputations themselves were often a source of infection—killing more than one-quarter of all soldiers who had limbs amputated. Surgeons operated in bloody aprons, with unwashed hands and unsterilized knives and saws. They moved from patient to patient using the same unwashed instruments. Nearly 60 percent of Civil War soldiers who had amputations at the knee—performed when the patient was fully conscious because doctors had no anesthetics—died. More than 80 percent died after hip-level amputations. Soldiers who survived often struggled to make a living after the procedure, especially if they farmed or worked with their hands.

Although neither Mary nor other doctors knew about germs at that time, her medical training had taught her the importance of good hygiene. She believed that many amputations could be avoided if doctors and nurses kept wounds clean and bandaged. She recalled one time assisting with the amputation of a man's arm. "The two surgeons in the ward who had decided to have that arm amputated when there had been only a slight flesh wound, seemed to me to take this opportunity to amputate for the purpose of their own practice," she wrote in her journal, "which was utterly cruel." But Mary knew that as a volunteer (and a woman at that), if she objected, she would be banned from the hospital. She kept quiet, and the surgeons removed the poor soldier's arm.

"I then made up my mind that it was the last case that would ever occur if it was in my power to prevent such cruel loss of limbs," Mary wrote. Afterward, whenever a soldier fearfully confided that he was scheduled for an amputation, she asked to see the wound. "In almost every instance," she wrote, "I saw amputation was not only unnecessary, but to me it just seemed wickedly cruel. I would then swear the soldier not to repeat anything that I told him, and then I would tell him that no one was obliged to submit to an amputation unless he chose to do so, that his limbs belonged to himself." If the surgeons insisted on amputation, she told the soldier, he should "declare that if they forced him to have an operation that he would never rest after his recovery until he had shot them dead." Mary found a way to decrease amputations without confronting the surgeons. She later pointed out that not only did she save many men from losing their limbs, but she also saved the government millions of dollars in pensions (support payments) that would have been made to the disabled men.

At one point, Dorothea Dix visited Indiana Hospital. The two women did not hit it off. Mary was appalled by what she called Dix's "sham modesty." As they walked through the hospital together, Mary noted that when Dix "saw a patient who was too ill to arrange the clothing on his cot if it became disarranged and a foot was exposed she turned her head the other way seeming not to see the condition while I was so disgusted with such sham modesty that I hastened to arrange the soldier's clothing if I chanced to be near when no nurses were to do this duty."

Mary said that Dix seemed "troubled" upon meeting her. She later learned that Dix had a policy of hiring only women over the age of thirty but not older than fifty, and only those who dressed in plain, drab colors. She didn't want any flirtatious behavior between the nurses and the soldiers. Dix most certainly did not think that Mary, who was an attractive twenty-eight-year-old, belonged in a hospital filled with men. It's safe to assume that Dix did not approve of Mary's trousers, either.

Mary wore a modified uniform during her service for the Union army. Her skirt was slightly longer than the men's uniform coats.

Dix's insistence on hiring only plain-looking older women stymied the dreams of many women who wanted to join the war effort as nurses because they were either too young or too good-looking. Jane Woolsey, another Civil War nurse, wryly observed, "Society just now presents the unprecedented spectacle of many women trying to make-believe that they are over thirty!"

Mary did concede that Dix was a "good hearted woman" who had performed a "great service in [homes for the mentally ill] where she helped do away with cruelties to patients," and for this "the country should be grateful to her."

Mary found her work rewarding, but by January 1862 the lack of a commission and her disagreement with the methods used to treat wounded soldiers led her to enroll in a course of study at the Hygeio-Therapeutic College in New York City. The college emphasized good sanitation, nutrition, exercise, and water therapies in the treatment of patients. And, just as important for Mary, it enthusiastically accepted women. Her friend and fellow dress reform advocate Lydia Sayer Hasbrouck had graduated from the college. After just three months of study, Mary was awarded a medical certificate on March 31, 1862.

In July of that year, Mary wrote a letter to the *Sibyl*, urging women to stand firm on the issue of dress reform. She called out women, including prominent suffragists, who had abandoned clothing reform because they had been criticized or ridiculed.

Mary returned to Oswego in October and gave a series of public lectures on her experiences at the Indiana Hospital and her impressions of the nation's capital. The owners of the lecture venue paid Mary for her lectures, so they subsidized her unpaid work as a war surgeon. In her handwritten notes for a lecture titled "On Washington," she describes the capital's streets, landscape, and buildings in great detail, calling the city beautiful. But Mary wanted her listeners to know what slavery had done to the soul of the city—and the country. Noting that it was founded as the nation's capital in 1790, she exclaimed, "What changes have been wrought in the last 72 years!, & had not slavery cursed our land, there would have been still greater strides visible here, in the march of civilization and everything good that is connected with it."

Mary could not stay away from the war for long. She moved back to Washington, DC, in early November. The midterm election was coming up, and the antislavery Republicans needed to keep control of Congress to carry out their wartime agenda. One day she walked past a building where a group of soldiers had gathered. They were waiting in line to fill out the necessary travel documents so they could return home to vote. Seeing that the office was overwhelmed with travel requests, she pushed her way through the crowds and volunteered to stay until midnight to help with the paperwork. In a poignant reminder of the struggle for women's suffrage, she later remarked, "I helped others to vote if not allowed to myself."

Mary learned that there were many sick and wounded soldiers in nearby Warrenton, Virginia, where General Ambrose Burnside was the commander, and volunteered her services. She was shocked to find the soldiers lying on the floor of an old house, with no trained medical officers to care for them. Many of the men were gravely ill with typhoid fever, an infectious disease spread through food or water contaminated by the bacteria *Salmonella typhi* or through close contact with someone already infected. The military officer in charge had been trying to take care of the patients while readying able-bodied men in his charge to head for Richmond the next day. "For God's sake," he implored her, "do something for [the sick] if you can."

Mary's recent training in hygiene served her well. She knew it was critical to keep the men clean, but the only supplies available to her were a bucket of water and a single cup. She went in search of something—anything—to help her care for the men and found that the Confederate army had taken everything of value from nearby homes. Finally, she found a washbasin that one woman had managed to hide from the soldiers. Mary bought it from the woman for one silver dollar of her own money—the equivalent of twenty-seven dollars in modern times.

Ambrose Burnside had served during the Mexican-American War (1846–1848) as a second lieutenant. When the Civil War broke out, he organized the First Rhode Island Infantry Regiment, which marched to DC to protect the capital.

Lacking any towels or washcloths to bathe the men or to make warm compresses, Mary had a brilliant idea. She tore her only nightdress into pieces about a foot square (0.09 sq. m) to make towels and distributed one to each soldier. The public was shocked at her seeming lack of modesty. One writer scornfully remarked, "[Walker] started out fighting typhoid, scurvy, and diarrhea with the Army of the Potomac; in 1862, she was tearing up her nighties to make wet compresses for the soldiers." Mary didn't care what polite society thought. She instructed a healthy soldier to wash the faces and hands of those who were too sick to wash themselves and to use clean water for each man.

Mary knew that the men needed better care than she could provide them in this makeshift hospital. She went to General Burnside and asked that her patients be sent to Washington, DC, where they could be properly cared for. On November 15, 1862, General Burnside personally signed an order authorizing Mary to escort the sick troops to Washington, DC.

She and her patients boarded a train with six freight cars and one passenger car, which carried men on official business, including US senator Henry Wilson of Massachusetts, who would later become Ulysses S. Grant's vice president. The sick and injured men were packed into the freight cars, with some men even riding on top of the train.

The train went only a short distance when it stopped. While they were waiting for the train to start moving again, Mary took the opportunity to check on her patients. Two of them were near death. "As I approached one I saw that he was near the other shore," she recalled, "and asked him his name, which I wrote down, but before I could get anything more except his regiment, he had passed to the beyond." The other man could barely speak his name, and she had to guess what he was trying to say. Mary recorded the names so she could tell the men's families how they had died. She considered it essential to give the family a "history of the brave life and death of the soldier, signing my full name."

When the train failed to continue, Mary became impatient with the delay and asked the conductor what was going on. He told her that he lacked the authorization to make the trip to DC. She showed him General Burnside's letter and commanded him to proceed. "I could not help suppressing a smile," she wrote, "at the thought of his stating that he was waiting for orders, and that in reality I was then military conductor of the train. . . . Since then it has been with some pride that I have recalled the fact that I have been the conductor of a train that had conveyed the future Vice President of the United States."

Mary had earned General Burnside's trust and respect in Warrenton, and he used his influence to help her gain access to other battlefield hospitals. The Union army had been gravely defeated in a battle in Fredericksburg, Virginia, almost 60 miles (96 km) south of Washington, DC, in December 1862. There were nearly thirteen thousand casualties, and by all accounts, their suffering was dreadful. Walt Whitman, who had already become famous as the poet who wrote *Leaves of Grass* in 1855, came to a makeshift hospital in a mansion in Fredericksburg to look for his brother George. He saw "a heap of feet, legs, arms, and human fragments, cut, bloody, black and blue, swelled and sickening." Dead bodies were lined up in the garden, "each covered with its brown woollen blanket." Whitman found his brother, whose injuries were minor, but he was so moved by the soldiers' plight that he volunteered to work as a nurse, which he wrote about in his poem "The Wound-Dresser":

Thus in silence in dreams' projections,
Returning, resuming, I thread my way through the
hospitals,
The hurt and wounded I pacify with soothing hand,
I sit by the restless all the dark night, some are so young,
Some suffer so much, I recall the experience sweet
and sad,
(Many a soldier's loving arms about this neck have
cross'd and rested,
Many a soldier's kiss dwells on these bearded lips.)

Clara Barton's service during the Civil War earned her the nickname Angel of the Battlefield. In addition to founding the American Red Cross, she worked at the new Missing Soldiers Office to reconnect soldiers with their families.

The military surgeons told Mary to take any cases she chose at Fredericksburg and to ready them to travel to DC. Mary did not mention meeting Whitman at the Fredericksburg hospital, but it would not be surprising if she had. It is likely that at the hospital she did meet and work alongside Clara Barton, another famous Civil War nurse, who would go on to found the American Red Cross. Barton worked tirelessly in Fredericksburg, tending to the needs of so many patients that she later wrote, "I wrung the blood from the bottom of my clothing, before I could step, for the weight about my feet."

Mary's many acts of kindness to soldiers and their families show that she was a caring doctor, but in her journals, she also noted with clinical fascination some of the more horrific wounds suffered by the soldiers:

Among these cases was a man where a shell had taken a part of his skull away, about as large a piece as a dollar, although not the same shape. I could see the pulsation of the brain, and when he talked I could see a movement of the same, slight though it was. He was perfectly sensible, and although I never saw him again after he was taken to Washington, I learned that he lived several days.

Mary continued her work at battlefield hospitals throughout the winter and spring of 1863, although she also found time to travel back to Washington, DC, and New York. On January 1, 1863, President Lincoln signed the Emancipation Proclamation, an executive order declaring that all enslaved people in the Confederacy "shall be then, thenceforward, and forever free." The executive order did not free enslaved people in states loyal to the Union; it was a war measure meant to cripple the Confederacy by robbing it of free Black labor and by allowing Black people to serve in the Union army. Official freedom for enslaved people did not come until the Thirteenth Amendment to the Constitution was ratified—or approved by the states—nearly two years later.

Mary traveled to New York to celebrate with other abolitionists in February 1863, but she soon moved back to DC. Since the beginning of the war, Mary had been working for the military without pay. While in the field, she received food rations and a tent to sleep in. She took steps to proclaim her role as a military medical officer. She donned a green sash reserved for surgeons and a dark blue uniform typically worn by officers. "I had not then any government authority to do so," Mary later wrote. In typical Mary fashion, she gave herself that authority.

In DC, Mary made a meager living writing for the *Sibyl*, lecturing, and perhaps seeing a few private patients. She was moved by the plight of women who had come to the city looking for their wounded fathers, husbands, and sons. One day she noted a pool of blood on the sidewalk by the Treasury Building. A police officer told her that a woman had fallen there and had been taken to the police station. Mary learned that the woman, who was pregnant with her first child, had come to the capital in search of her husband. Although Mary did not go into detail in her journal, it seems likely that the woman had had a miscarriage. "She had walked until she was nearly dead," Mary related, "trying to get accommodation in a hotel and had failed. She had then made efforts and pleaded to be taken into some private house where she had money to pay her expenses, but that none would allow her to stop with them." It's likely that the woman was shunned because prostitutes were numerous in the city, so any unaccompanied women were greeted with suspicion. People probably assumed that this woman, too, was a prostitute and therefore refused to help her.

Mary was determined to help this woman and others like her. A few evenings later, she made an appeal at a local women's suffrage meeting to raise funds for a "respectable" women's lodging. With the money she collected, she rented a house. She talked an army officer into donating cots, blankets, bed linens, and kitchenware from the army's commissary (supply room). Ever resourceful, Mary asked him "for those things that for any reason were condemned as not being fit for soldier's hospitals, if they were torn or needed repairing, or if they needed cleansing by washing, and if cots were not stout enough for heavy soldiers or had been a little broken I would see that they were all fixed and suitable for a woman's home."

To keep the shelter going, Mary recruited volunteers for a new organization, the Women's Relief Association. She worked for two months as the association's secretary, a member of the finance committee, and physician, an experience that reinforced her passion for helping the poor, particularly women.

Mary met President Lincoln and his wife, Mary Todd Lincoln, at a reception that spring, where she described the president as "cordial" and the First Lady as "lively and pleasing." She would later encounter Lincoln under less pleasant circumstances, which she recounted in an article for the *Oswego Times*. The president was among those waiting for the arrival of a group of Confederate prisoners captured in a battle at Chancellorsville, Virginia. She noted the drops of sweat rolling down his "careworn cheeks" and described the misery of the captured soldiers: "Some had no shoes or stockings; some no coats, and nothing but a woolen shirt about their waists."

The Battle of Gettysburg, which raged for three days at the beginning of July 1863 in Pennsylvania, was a victory for the Union army and a turning point in the war. It came at a terrible cost to both sides: 3,155 Union soldiers and 3,903 Confederate soldiers lost their lives. More than 33,000 soldiers were wounded, and nearly 11,000 went missing. Mary arrived at Gettysburg after the battle was over and accompanied the soldiers on their long trip back to DC. Able-bodied men were required to march in the sweltering July heat, and several soldiers died of sunstroke. She gave up her place in the wagon for exhausted soldiers and carried equipment for them while she was riding.

★ ★ ★

Mary returned to the battlefield in September 1863, working in a hospital in Chattanooga, Tennessee, where her medical and organizational skills brought her to the attention of General George H. Thomas. In the months to come, Thomas would become Mary's champion when she most needed one. The surgeon in charge of the hospital, Dr. Francis Salter, asked Mary to continue working for him, but she wanted an official appointment. She came up with a bold plan: she wrote to Secretary of War Edwin Stanton, asking for permission to raise a regiment of men to be called "Walker's US Patriots." She would serve as the regiment's first assistant surgeon: "Having been so long the friend of soldiers . . . I feel confident that I can be successful in getting re-enlistment of men who would not enlist in any other persons Reg[iment]."

She learned in January 1864 that her proposal had been rejected. Undaunted, Mary appealed directly to President Lincoln. In a letter addressed "To His Excellency," she wrote that she had been denied a commission solely on the basis of her sex. Writing about herself in the third person, Mary stated, "She fully believes that had a man been as useful to our country as she modestly claims to have been, a star would have been taken from the National Heavens and placed upon his shoulder."

But Lincoln also turned her down. He knew that giving Mary a commission would cause a great deal of controversy, and he wasn't willing to take it on.

Frustrated, Mary decided to return to the hospital in Chattanooga, where the medical team had respected her and her work. There, Mary encountered an unusual patient—Frank Miller. Miller, a soldier from Illinois, had been captured by the Confederate army the previous fall and shot in the leg in an attempted escape. While doctors were treating the wound, they discovered that Miller was in fact a woman. Miller had ended up in Chattanooga as part of a prisoner exchange. Mary wrote that Miller's story was "a singular case of female martial [military] spirit and patriotic devotion to the flag" and convinced the woman to talk to reporters. Miller told the story of how she and her brother, both orphans, had enlisted in the spring of 1861. Her brother had been killed the following year.

Frances Hook was one of multiple women who disguised themselves as men to serve in the army during the Civil War. After healing from her injuries, Hook joined another regiment, still dressed as a man. She was once again discovered when she was captured and imprisoned by the Confederates in Atlanta, Georgia.

Frank Miller admitted that her name was really Frances Hook and allowed photographers to take her picture. She said that when Confederate president Jefferson Davis learned of her real identity, he offered her a lieutenant's commission if she defected to the South. Hook declined, telling Davis that she "preferred to fight as a private soldier for the stars and stripes [Union], rather than be honored with a commission from the Rebs [rebels]."

Mary thought that the Union army should take a cue from Davis. She told a reporter that "Congress should assign women to duty in the army, with compensation," noting that "patriotism has no sex." Instead, the army discharged Hook and sent her home.

In March 1864, Assistant Surgeon General Robert Wood, who had long been sympathetic to Mary's cause, directed her to report to Chattanooga for an army medical board exam to evaluate her skills as a physician. She appeared before a board of medical officers, presenting them with her degree from Syracuse Medical College, her certificate from Hygeio-Therapeutic College, and several letters of recommendation.

After evaluating her skills and knowledge, the board issued an assessment dripping with scorn, saying that she "betrayed such utter ignorance of any subject in the whole range of medical science . . . she had no more medical knowledge than an ordinary housewife, that she was, of course, entirely unfit for the position of medical officer, and that she might be made useful as a nurse."

Sexism surely played a large role in the medical officers' evaluation, but they were also conventional physicians who dismissed her beliefs in the importance of hygiene and water therapy as unproven and unsound medicine. Mary was furious and would later say that the entire examination was a farce, with "more than half the time consumed in questions regarding subjects that were exclusively feminine & had no sort of relation to the wounds and diseases of soldiers."

Then Mary appealed directly to her friend General Thomas. On March 14, 1864, Thomas overruled the board's rejection. He appointed her as a surgeon for the Fifty-Second Ohio Volunteers, stationed at Gordon's Mills, near Chattanooga. Mary's persistence had finally paid off.

CHAPTER 4

CONTRACT CIVILIAN ASSISTANT SURGEON

IN MARCH 1864, DR. MARY E. WALKER, holding the position "contract civilian assistant surgeon," reported for duty at Gordon's Mills, Georgia, just across the border from Chattanooga. She would be paid eighty dollars a month and given a horse and saddle. She reported to Colonel Daniel McCook Jr., who welcomed her with respect and confidence in her abilities. Mary would later describe McCook as "a man of great sympathy and a large sense of justice."

She slept in the kitchen of the miller Gordon and his family. McCook and his officers slept in another room down the hall—an arrangement that was deemed respectable for a young single woman. She continued to wear her modified bloomer uniform, with the green sash of a medical doctor, but made one significant change to her appearance to celebrate her gender: "I let my curls grow while I was in the army so that everybody would know I was a woman."

McCook gave Mary a great deal of authority—something that not all his men appreciated. One day McCook asked Mary to don a red officer's sash and review, or formally inspect, the guards on horseback. Mary later noted with pride, "This is the only instance in the war, as far as I knew, where a woman made a revue." McCook's men groused and gossiped about Mary's and McCook's relationship. They believed a woman could not gain that sort of power without being intimate with her superior.

The medical duties at Gordon's Mills were fairly light—most of the severely injured men had been sent to nearby hospitals. So Colonel McCook encouraged Mary to travel beyond Union lines to treat local citizens. She learned that all the physicians in the area had been forced into service for the Confederate army, leaving the locals in dire need of a doctor. While the colonel could not order her to enter Confederate territory—a dangerous proposition for any Union doctor, male or female—she often did so, accompanied by two officers and two orderlies, all of them armed. In addition to her medical kit, Mary carried two revolvers in her saddlebags.

One afternoon the family of a sick child came to Gordon's Mills, begging for a doctor. The family lived several miles away in a dangerous part of the country. McCook decided he couldn't risk losing his officers to accompany her when he had so few at headquarters. But Mary was not dissuaded: "As they begged so hard for a physician I stated to General McCook that I would go alone and relieve that distress if he would not allow any one to go with me. . . . As General McCook was a man of great sympathy and large sense of justice, he said that if I so much desired that he would allow two of the officers and two orderlies to go with me."

Women's hair during the Civil War was often styled in long curls or fastened to the head in a bun. Mary's more feminine long curls would help her convince suspicious people that she was a woman despite her unusual dress.

When Mary arrived at the family's home, she found the toddler had tetanus, a disease of the nervous system that in that era usually led to a painful death. She recalled in her journal, "I knew that there was but one chance in a very large number of its recovery, and when I thought of my remaining there so far from headquarters, where there was but one woman, and that the young mother . . . and four or five men in the house, I felt a little afraid to stay." She gave the mother instructions on how to care for the child and said that she would try to return the next day. She and her escorts raced back to the safety of the Union headquarters, hoping to arrive before dark. Unfortunately, McCook was unwilling to allow his officers or Mary to return to the home, and she never found out what happened to the child.

It was abundantly clear to Mary that being a woman *and* a Yankee in enemy territory was perilous. But at some point she began to travel without her escorts, who had other duties. Later, she wrote, "The people expressed so much gratitude that I lost all fear of anything being done to me." She described one close call that took place about 3 miles (4.8 km) from Union headquarters. She was traveling alone without her revolvers, believing that if Confederate soldiers searched her and discovered the weapons, she would be in a great deal of trouble. As she was passing an old barn, two Confederate soldiers emerged and ordered her to stop. They asked where she was going, and Mary said she was going to see patients. One of the soldiers, realizing she was with the Union army, ordered her to drive her wagon into the barn. "I very coolly asked him what for," she wrote in her journal, "and then said that I was in a hurry to get to that patient." After some back and forth, the two men said that she could continue on her journey.

When Mary returned to headquarters, she "spoke of this little adventure," describing the leader of the two men in detail. The officers jumped to their feet. He sounded just like the notorious Champ Ferguson, who had sworn to kill every Yankee who crossed his path. "A good many years later," Mary wrote, "I saw a picture of that very man, which I recognized immediately, and I was so faint with the very thought of how narrowly I escaped death that I could hardly stand up." Still, the confrontation did not stop Mary from seeking out new people to help.

Mary's patients were grateful for her services, but her style of dress baffled them. How could a woman possibly dress like a man? It just wasn't done! The mother of the child with tetanus called her "Sir." In another case, Mary treated a sick old woman who lived with her daughter. The woman asked Mary to spend the night but said she would have to share a bed with her daughter. It was common for family members and visitors of the same gender to share a bed, and so the two women bunked together.

Then Mary treated a very sick young man, who soon recovered. "I suddenly became very famous in that neighborhood," she told a reporter. "Exaggerated accounts of my skill and learning . . . reached the ears of the old lady just mentioned." On her next visit to the old woman, Mary asked for the same sleeping arrangement.

The woman hesitated and then stated, "Look here, I'm afeared of you; I'm afeared to let you sleep with my daughter again, for I am afeared you ain't a woman; I don't believe any woman could know as much about doctoring folks as you do."

So Mary let down her hair. Shaking it on her shoulders, she said "Look there, did you ever see a man have such hair as that?" She asked the mother to pull on her hair as hard as she liked to make sure it was really attached to her head. The mother did so, and once again, Mary had a sleeping mate for the night.

Mary had another motive for her frequent forays into enemy territory: to serve as a spy for the Union army, although she only hinted at it in her writings. In September 1862, she wrote a letter to the secretary of war, offering her services as a spy:

> *I again offer my services to my country. . . . I refer to my being sent to Richmond under a "flag of truce" for the relief of our sick soldiers and then use the style (of double communication [code] in writing their necessities) that I invented, to give you information as [to] their forces plans and any important information. No one knows what the style of writing is, except Hon. Mssrs. Cameron Seward and Mr. Allen of the "Secret Service." . . . Any "secret service" that your Hon. Body may wish performed will find in me one eminently fitted to do it.*

"Mr. Allen" was none other than Allan Pinkerton of the Pinkerton National Detective Agency. Before the Civil War, Pinkerton had realized that women could often infiltrate social gatherings and collect information that no man could obtain and hired a number of female operatives. Pinkerton's first female agent, Kate Warne, was able to befriend the wife of a respected man accused of stealing thousands of dollars from his employer and got her to confess that her husband had indeed stolen the money and buried it under their cellar floor. President Lincoln

Left to right: Allan Pinkerton is shown here with President Lincoln and Major General John McClernand at a Union camp in Antietam, Maryland. During the war, Pinkerton used an alias, Major E. J. Allan, to hide his identity, which may be why Mary referred to him as "Mr. Allen" instead of "Mr. Pinkerton."

had authorized Pinkerton to establish a secret service to gather intelligence about Confederate military activities.

Like any good spy, Mary was tight-lipped about her acts of espionage, but General Thomas would later admit that he assigned her to the Fifty-Second Ohio Volunteers so that she could act as a spy. Being stationed so close to Confederate territory meant that Mary would have access to important information from the opposing army. After the war, the public learned that she had "gained information that led [Union] General [William Tecumseh] Sherman to so modify his strategic operations as to save himself from a serious reverse and obtain success where defeat before seemed to be inevitable."

Mary knew that spying for the Union army was fraught with danger. So it might not have come as a surprise to her when Confederate soldiers arrested her on suspicion of espionage on April 10, 1864, when she was thirty-one years old and making her rounds in enemy territory. Details of her arrest are sketchy, but one Confederate soldier later recalled that "she rode boldly up to our picket [guard] and asked if he would take some letters which she wished delivered within our lines"— leading some historians to speculate that she intentionally provoked her capture in an attempt to gather valuable information inside a Confederate military prison. Mary, true to form, did not let the soldiers see her fear, telling them she would be glad to rest her weary limbs.

Five days after her capture, General Grant, presumably fearing the discovery of the military's use of women spies, ordered all women to leave Union battlefield areas. Mary's captors took her to Dalton, Georgia, where Benedict Semmes, a Confederate captain who witnessed her arrival, later said, "We were all amused and disgusted too at the sight of a *thing* that nothing but the debased and the depraved Yankee nation could produce—'a female doctor.'" Semmes pronounced her "not good looking and of course had tongue enough for a regiment of men."

She was soon sent to the notorious Castle Thunder Prison in Richmond, Virginia. Brigadier General William M. Gardner, the Confederate commander of all military prisons in the East, took charge of her case. The plan was to exchange her for a Confederate prisoner as soon as possible. Gardner said that Mary was "the most personable and gentlemanly looking young woman" he had ever seen and even suggested to her that she might have gotten away with her spying if she had worn women's clothing.

Castle Thunder Prison was originally a tobacco warehouse before the outbreak of the Civil War. It was set up as a military prison in 1862 under the command of George W. Alexander and quickly gained a reputation as one of the most brutal Confederate prisons.

Mary spent the next four months of her life at Castle Thunder. The infamous prison, which held Union political prisoners (people held in prison for their political activity) and spies, Confederate deserters, people charged with treason, and a few prostitutes, was located in a tobacco warehouse and had a reputation of being brutal, overcrowded, and filthy. It was overrun by insects and rats, and its inmates suffered from illnesses ranging from pneumonia to malnutrition. There was never enough food, and the little they had was often moldy or filled with maggots. Upon Mary's arrival at Castle Thunder, she learned that another female spy had recently been drugged, raped, and killed by three of the prison officers. Guards routinely harassed her.

Mary managed to send a letter to her parents from Castle Thunder, which they had published in a northern newspaper. Not wanting to worry them, she spun a splendid lie about conditions in the prison:

> *I hope you are not grieving about me because I am a prisoner-of-war. I am living in a three-story brick castle with plenty to eat and a clean bed to sleep in. I have a room-mate, a young lady about 20 years of age, from near Corinth, Miss. I am much happier than I might be in some relations of life, where I might be envied by other ladies. The officers are gentlemanly and kind, and it will not be long before I am exchanged.*

She did her best to boost the spirits of her fellow Union prisoners as well. More than one prisoner told the story of seeing a petite woman standing at the window of her cell, cooling herself with a fan displaying the American flag. It was her way of telling them, "I'm with you. We can survive this."

The Richmond newspapers delighted in mocking this Yankee woman surgeon who was "ugly and skinny, apparently above 30 years of age," and who wore "full male costume." Mary didn't care about the insults regarding her personal appearance, but she couldn't let the remark about her clothing go.

She wrote a letter to the editor of the *Richmond Dispatch* in response: "Simple justice demands correction. I am attired in what is usually called the 'bloomer' or 'reform dress,' which is similar to other ladies, with the exception of its being shorter and more physiological [appropriate for health] than long dresses."

Other reporters claimed, without evidence, that she had an affair with another prisoner, got into a hair-pulling fight with one of her roommates, and spent her time "devouring all the novel nonsense and trash she can get hold of with a negro character in them." The latter claim may well have been true; Mary was keenly interested in the lives of enslaved Black people.

Predictably, Mary kept herself busy during her time in prison. She volunteered to care for sick prisoners in Castle Thunder, but prison officials turned her down. So she undertook some clever freelance doctoring. A man "connected with the prison" asked for her help to avoid being drafted into the Confederate army. She prepared a mixture of chopped apples and red pepper and instructed him to eat it and run around before reporting for his medical examination. Presumably the combination of hot peppers and running made his heart race. He was given a diagnosis of the "worst disease of the heart," and that was that. No military service for him. Mary also wrote letters for other prisoners asking for their release. In one case she even succeeded in persuading Jefferson Davis to pardon a Confederate soldier sentenced to death for desertion.

At last, on August 12, 1864, Mary was released as part of a prisoner exchange negotiated by the Union and Confederate armies. Both sides needed physicians, and she was exchanged for a Confederate surgeon from Tennessee. Reportedly, she shouted "Huzzah!" as she left the prison. She may have been in good spirits as she left the prison, but physically she was weak. She would later say that at one point she had been near starvation. The gas-burning lamps in her cell and throughout the prison had damaged her eyes, and during her imprisonment she developed an eye infection. Her eyesight was never the same.

THE INVALID CORPS

When the Civil War began, the Union army thought the war would be over in a year. It was not worried about running out of troops, so it allowed soldiers to return home if they were injured in battle. As the war dragged on, though, the Union began to run low on troops. Officers were desperate for men to work behind the lines: escorting prisoners of war; guarding cities, supply depots, and railroads; working in hospitals and kitchens; and doing clerical work. To fill these jobs, in 1863 the War Department created the Invalid Corps, made up of disabled soldiers who could no longer fight on the front lines. One recruitment poster read,

**MEN WANTED
FOR THE
INVALID CORPS.**

Only those faithful soldiers who, from wounds or the hardships of war, are no longer fit for duty will be received in this Corps of Honor. Enlistments will be for three years, unless sooner discharged. Pay and allowances same as for officers and men of the United States Infantry.

Men who joined the Invalid Corps had been honorably discharged for their war injuries, yet some derided them as cowards or shirkers who were trying to dodge their patriotic duty to serve on the front lines. One jeering song went like this:

I wanted much to go to war,
And went to be examined;

The surgeon looked me o'er and o'er,
My back and chest he hammered.
Said he, you're not the man for me,
Your lungs are much affected,
And likewise both your eyes are cock'd,
And otherwise defected.

So now I'm with the invalids,
And cannot go and fight, sir!
The doctor told me so, you know,
Of course it must be right, sir!

Members of the corps faced such ridicule on a daily basis. Their sky blue uniforms set them apart from the regular army's dark blue uniforms. Even the name Invalid Corps came to evoke shame and stigma, since the military had previously used the

The Invalid Corps was set up much the same as a normal military unit with the typical ranks and officers. They even had a drum corps such as the one pictured here.

initials "I.C." to stamp items considered damaged and substandard. The initials stood for "Inspected, Condemned."

The Invalid Corps was put to the test in July 1864. A Confederate force of fifteen thousand troops was making its way north to Maryland in a desperate attempt to take Washington, DC. General Ulysses S. Grant had sent a large number of soldiers to mount a campaign more than 100 miles (161 km) from DC. All that was left to defend the capital were clerks, government officials, and the Invalid Corps stationed at Fort Stevens, 3 miles (4.8 km) away. President Lincoln himself went to Fort Stevens to watch as Confederate troops launched an attack there.

Captain James O'Beirne had joined the Invalid Corps after a bullet had ricocheted off his head, another bullet had lodged in his leg, and he had been shot in the chest in battle. His right arm was paralyzed. At Fort Stevens, he stood with Lincoln on the ramparts, a defensive wall surrounding the fort, as bullets roared around them. O'Beirne and the rest of the Invalid Corps defended the capital and the president from the Confederates for twenty-four hours, until regular Union troops arrived to help. (O'Bierne, along with other Union soldiers, later tracked down John Wilkes Booth after Lincoln's assassination.)

After the Fort Stevens attack, soldiers in the Invalid Corps pushed back against its name and uniform. Later that year, the War Department renamed it the Veterans Corps. Members were supplied with regulation dark blue uniforms. The corps recruited more than sixty thousand men during its three-year existence.

Mary returned to Washington, DC, with little more than the clothes on her back. The army granted her five months' back pay. She met with President Lincoln, at his request, to describe the conditions at Castle Thunder. This time, she told the truth about her experiences in that terrible prison. She briefly thought about returning to private practice, but her sense of duty and her desire to make her mark in a man's world sent her back to the military.

In early September 1864, Mary headed south to meet up with her colleagues from the Fifty-Second Ohio Volunteers in Louisville, Kentucky. She learned that her friend, ally, and former commanding officer Colonel McCook had died after being seriously wounded storming the Confederate front lines, shouting, "Surrender, you traitors!"

Shortly after, while in Louisville, Mary drafted a letter to General Sherman, asking once again to be given a commission in the army. Shrewdly, she asked to be appointed surgeon of the female prisoners and female refugees in Louisville. How could they argue that it was improper for a woman to treat other women? "I have but to remind you," she wrote, "that there has not been a Woman who has served Government in such a variety of ways of importance to the great *Cause* which has elicited patriotism that knows no sex."

General Sherman approved the appointment but not the commission. Still, it was an official paid position, and Mary accepted with one request: that she be given a twenty-day leave to return to Oswego. Sherman granted her request with the option of applying for an extension beyond twenty days. He knew that the reason for her leave was not personal but political:

Mary wanted to campaign on behalf of President Lincoln in the upcoming election, which was to be held on November 8. While on leave, she spoke at rallies in support of Lincoln, the Republican candidate.

After Lincoln won reelection, Mary headed back to Louisville to take up her new job as surgeon in charge of the Female Military Prison. Her patients were Confederate women and sometimes their children. Some were prostitutes, some were longtime criminals, but most were there for their actions during the war such as spying or aiding enemy forces. None, not surprisingly, were happy about being imprisoned, and many took an immediate disliking of this Yankee woman doctor. One prisoner later recalled, "The anomalous [unusual] creature that was put over us for our sins and I remember lying in a half stupor and wondering what the *thing* was. The dress was that of a man, but the braided hair and skinny, shrewish features were those of a woman. Bitter experience soon taught me to know this *thing* well, for it was a woman—the prison doctor."

Mary's unpopularity was in part due to the fact that the physician she replaced, Dr. Erasmus O. Brown, resented having a woman in a position of power and did his best to poison her reputation with the prisoners. He continued to visit and treat patients, despite Mary's objections. She wrote a letter complaining about Dr. Brown's actions that made its way to the assistant surgeon general: "He has prejudiced . . . the inmates, and informed them that they were not to have anyone to prescribe for them but himself *if they did not choose to have another*, and told them that they were not to obey any of the orders but those given by himself."

Dr. Brown's superiors ordered him to stay out of the women's prison, but the damage to Mary's reputation there had already been done. She made matters worse by being much stricter with the prisoners and staff members than Brown. She would not tolerate "Rebel songs or disloyal talk" or profanity. She had one prisoner handcuffed for two hours because she cursed at a guard and threatened her. She put an end to "familiarity" between the female patients and the male guards—a polite way of saying that prisoners were exchanging sexual favors with staff members—and replaced four male cooks with female cooks. She insisted that the women keep themselves and their cells clean and threatened to remove custody from mothers or caretakers who abused their children.

One of Mary's loyal orderlies, Cary Conklin, later defended the doctor. Referring to a lieutenant who had complained about Mary, she wrote,

> *Dr. Walker had the entire professional charge of the prisoners and the guard, and was always kind and attentive to both—So much so to the prisoners, that some of the union people were very much displeased. The Lieut. commanding the guard seemed to take every opportunity, and study to do whatever he thought would annoy and make the position of the Surgeon in Charge a very trying one.*

In March 1865, the post's medical director recommended that Mary be relieved from duty. Although he had a good opinion of her, he understood that this post was not a good fit for either the doctor or her charges. Mary, in turn, had had her fill of the post. The day after learning of her dismissal, she wrote to the director: "It has been an untold task to keep this institution in a good condition *morally* & I am weary of the task &

would much prefer to be where my services can be appreciated & I [can] do more good *directly* for the Cause."

A few weeks later, on April 9, Confederate general Robert E. Lee surrendered and Union general Ulysses S. Grant proclaimed, "The war is over. The rebels are our countrymen again."

Mary moved on to the Union's Refugee House in Clarksville, Tennessee. She served as director there from April 11 to May 17, 1865. It was a haven for people whose lives had been turned upside down by the war. Most of her new charges were desperately poor, trying to get home after fleeing the war's violence. The same day that Mary began work at the Refugee House, President Lincoln gave a speech to a mostly enthusiastic crowd from the balcony of the White House. For the first, time, he made public his belief that some Black people—only men—should be given the right to vote: "It is unsatisfactory to some that the elective franchise is not given to the colored man," he said. "I would myself prefer that it were now conferred on the very intelligent, and on those who serve our cause as soldiers."

President Lincoln's final address was the catalyst for his assassination. A crowd gathered outside the White House calling for the president, and he gave his speech that evening. In addition to announcing his support for suffrage for Black people, Lincoln outlined his plan for bringing the country back together after the war.

This was hardly a ringing endorsement for universal voting rights for Black people, but it was a start. At least one of his audience members was *not* cheering. Confederate sympathizer and actor John Wilkes Booth, upon hearing his words, said to his companion, "That means [Black] citizenship! Now, by God, I'll put him through. That is the last speech he will ever make."

Three days later, Booth made good on his word. He assassinated Lincoln at Ford's Theatre in Washington, DC, as the president watched a play.

On Easter Sunday, just two days after Lincoln's assassination, Mary attended a church service at the Trinity Episcopal Church in Clarksville, TN. She wore her Union uniform with a short skirt, which of course horrified many people in the congregation. Many churchgoers had painted their Easter lilies black in mourning for the slain president. Not at this church. At the front, she saw a flower arrangement of white lilies with a single red geranium. She thought it was a quiet tribute to the fallen Confederacy. She cut off the blue ribbon from her dagger and placed it on the arrangement, a silent tribute to the American flag.

The minister was not pleased! He removed the ribbon and finished the service. She decided to attend that evening's church service, placing a small bouquet and an American flag at the front of the church. But the minister moved her bouquet and beloved flag aside. Furious, Mary rose from her seat and put them back where she had placed them. Nothing more was said, but the local newspapers breathlessly reported on the incident. One letter writer, identified only as "An Episcopalian," wrote "We do not know whether Major Walker considers herself a lady or not. Judging from her costume we would suppose not, and certainly no gentleman would so desecrate the House of God."

Not long after, Mary's superior, General George E. Cooper, relieved her of her duties at the Refugee House. The number of patients had dropped to the point where the doctor previously in charge of the hospital could care for them all.

Mary headed back to Washington, DC, where her war service officially ended. She collected the last of her pay and thought about her next steps. John Wilkes Booth had been found and killed, but news of the trial for his accomplices swirled around the capital. At the end of June, she returned to Richmond and triumphantly toured the dreadful Castle Thunder Prison as a free woman. She stayed in Richmond for the Independence Day celebration on July 4, 1865. Most of the crowd in the former capital of the Confederacy was subdued, with the exception of enthusiastic Union soldiers and those newly freed. Mary, dressed in her full blue surgeon's uniform for the last time, mounted the steps of Richmond's capitol building at the request of the event's organizers to read the Declaration of Independence.

Mary spent the next few weeks in New York City, where she befriended a "very fine woman" who was struggling to make ends meet. Mary didn't have much money of her own, so she cut her long hair, sold the curls (presumably to be used for wigs), and gave the money to the woman. She would never again feel the need to wear her curls long to make sure everyone knew she was a woman as she had during the war. She from then on wore her hair as it pleased her—whether cut short or pulled back in a bun.

It was around this time that Mary learned that her not-quite ex-husband, Albert Miller, had written to her brother-in-law Lyman Coats. With less than one year of the five-year waiting period left before the divorce could be finalized, he hoped they might get back together. "Can you tell me where Mary is?" he wrote. "I have not heard from her or of her in a long time. I think she will yet see that haste does not always lead to the right & regret our separation. I wish also to know if she is in need of any of the comforts or necessities of life. I would willingly assist her at any time, should she need it." What he did not mention in his letter was that he was still seeing several other women and had fathered more children. At any rate, Mary Walker had zero interest in reconciling with Albert Miller.

Much more welcome was the letter from Mary's old friend Lydia Sayer Hasbrouck. "Sister Walker, Where in the name of common sense are you to be found?" she gently teased. "We see your name here there & somewhere—but not one line from you this long time." Hasbrouck asked Mary to join her in upstate New York to work on behalf of women's suffrage and dress reform. She was planning a series of public lectures on those issues and wanted Mary to "help us as Sergeant Major to martial our forces."

Mary may have been tempted, but she wasn't quite done with the army. She decided to seek a postwar commission as an army surgeon at the Freedmen's Bureau in Washington, DC. The Freedmen's Bureau was established in March 1865, shortly before President Lincoln's death, to aid newly freed Black people, as well as thousands of war refugees and poor white farmers. Josephine Griffing, an abolitionist from Ohio, had persuaded President Lincoln to create the bureau, and she was hired as assistant to the assistant commissioner. Mary reasoned that if

One of the functions of the Freedmen's Bureau was to set up schools such as this one to help educate Black Americans.

one woman could be hired to work at the Freedmen's Bureau, surely the government would be willing to hire another.

What she didn't realize was that Griffing had been fired from her post earlier for criticizing the government's failure to address the hardships of former enslaved people. The new US president, Andrew Johnson, was not keen on outspoken women or on the well-being of Black Americans for that matter. Although he supported an end to slavery, he was a notorious white supremacist. A year later, he wrote, "This is a country for white men, and by God, as long as I am President, it shall be a government for white men." The last thing Johnson wanted to deal with was another strong woman who spoke her mind, especially one who championed the rights of Black people.

A larger issue was that Mary hoped that her commission would pave the way for other women who wanted to serve in the military. Military officials were well aware of her goal, and they didn't want to set such a precedent.

President Johnson asked the secretary of war if there was any way they could recognize Mary for her services. The president and his military advisers bandied about several options, including the possibility of giving her an honorary officer's title. They finally settled on the Medal of Honor, the highest award for military valor in action. Johnson's citation, dated November 11, 1865, noted that Mary "has devoted herself with much patriotic zeal to the sick and wounded soldiers, both in the field and hospitals, to the detriment of her own health, and has also endured hardships as a prisoner of war four months in a Southern prison while acting as a contract surgeon."

Mary was one of 1,522 people who received the Medal of Honor for service in the Civil War. She was the only female recipient of the award, a distinction she holds to this day. The medal immediately became her most prized possession. She wore it every day for the rest of her life.

Mary was photographed multiple times throughout her life. In many of the surviving photographs, she proudly wears her Medal of Honor on her lapel.

CHAPTER 5

POSTWAR ADVOCACY

THE LONG AND BLOODY WAR WAS OVER. The reunified nation was faced with the prospect of rebuilding. Mary had to do the same. She was just thirty-three years old and already famous. At first she tried to reestablish her medical practice in Washington, DC, but business was slow. Many people were still reluctant to see a female doctor—even a famous one—especially one who dressed in "men's" clothing. What's more, the damage to her eyesight made it impossible for her to perform surgery. With little money coming in from medicine, Mary had to find another way to earn a living.

Although she cherished her Medal of Honor, she understood that the government had used it to recognize her achievements without having to pay her the pension granted to men who served in the military. So in May 1866 Mary filed an appeal to the US Congress to be granted the pension she needed and deserved.

Mary still had plenty to keep her busy in between the too few patients who visited her office. War veterans, knowing that she had been a strong advocate for soldiers during the war, wrote her letters, hoping she could help them wade through the paperwork required to claim their own pensions. She attempted—without success—to get Congress to grant hundreds of female military nurses the same pensions and benefits awarded to male soldiers. The twenty dollars a month they sought, Mary told the press, was a "pitiable sum" for women who had "worn out their lives in our hospitals."

Some individuals just wanted to touch base with the famous doctor. One letter came from "a <u>very</u> young soldier that was in the rebel army & temporarily confined in <u>Castle Thunder</u>," as Mary wrote at the top of the letter after receiving it. He had been imprisoned in Castle Thunder while Mary was there, and there had been a little commotion in their part of the prison.

He wrote, "Do you remember the interest you took in me when I was called down one time and you thought I would be released? and do you remember how I found means to see you once more after I was released? I never forget any one or anything. . . . I remain as ever your Friend, G. Richmond."

Another former soldier sent her a picture of himself and wrote, "The press, had no other reason occurred, would have prevented me from forgetting you. It is with a mixture of curiosity and wonder that I watch your career and wonder where it will end."

Mary too must have wondered where her career would go from here. But in the meantime, she had to deal with Albert Miller. She had learned in November 1865 that Albert, who wanted to marry his longtime lover Delphine Freeman, had petitioned the New York Supreme Court to grant him a divorce from Mary! This was around the same time he had written to Mary's brother-in-law, supposedly wishing to reconcile with her—a sure indication that his intentions were less than honorable. Albert knew he could never legally remarry as the guilty party in Mary's divorce filing, so he decided to turn the tables on her. The court granted him the divorce, effectively tossing out Mary's own divorce petition. Mary was furious. To have him divorce her would be a stain on her reputation— something she could not tolerate.

She petitioned the New York State Assembly to overturn the court's decision. And on March 15, 1866, an assembly-man introduced "An Act for the relief of Mary E. Miller" to the assembly. As the senators debated the act, a newspaper in Utica reported on it, making her messy private life very public. The reporter scolded Mary for seeking special legislation to reverse Albert's divorce, writing that it "would soon make our divorce laws of no effect in guarding the sanctity of the marital relations."

The fact that the courts could throw out Mary's divorce petition and grant Albert a divorce instead was an example of discrimination against women—something Mary understood all too well. She wanted to make sure that divorce laws were fair for both men and women. Pursuing justice for herself made her even more determined to fight for the rights of all women.

It would take until January 2, 1869, for Mary's nine-year fight for a divorce to come to a close. The New York State Supreme Court determined that Mary's divorce petition had been wrongly dismissed and that Albert was the guilty party. Their marriage was dissolved, and Albert was barred from marrying again while Mary was alive. What the court didn't know was that Albert had already illegally married Delphine Freeman. When Mary received her official copy of the divorce decree, she put it in an envelope along with an old letter from Albert and wrote on the outside, "Divorce & Last Letter of the *Villain*."

Although Mary would receive several other marriage proposals over the years, she never accepted them. Since she dressed in men's clothing, some people speculated that she preferred women as romantic partners. Several years after her divorce, Mary received a letter from an angry California man whose wife, Dora, she had befriended. The husband accused Mary of meddling in their marital affairs and said that she had "gone so far [as] to occupy my bed and sleeping with my wife, a thing which, in consideration of the fact that your sex is questionable to say the least, imprudent." It was not uncommon in those days for women to sleep together as friends, but it's possible the two women were sexually involved.

In the years between the end of the war and the finalization of her divorce, Mary threw herself back into the women's rights movement. It was an especially thorny time for women's suffrage. Lawmakers were drafting the Fourteenth Amendment to the Constitution, which addressed citizenship rights and equal protection under the law. The first section of the amendment recognized "all persons born or naturalized [granted citizenship] in the United States" as citizens and forbade states from passing laws that would interfere with the privileges of citizenship. In other words, formerly enslaved Black Americans would be recognized as full citizens, with all the rights and protections of citizenship.

It was the proposed language in the second section of the amendment that alarmed Elizabeth Cady Stanton and other women suffragists. Lawmakers crafted it out of fear that southern states would not give Black people the right to vote. The amendment said that if a state denied the right to vote of "any of the male inhabitants of such State, being twenty-one years of age, and citizens of the United States," then its representation in Congress would be decreased.

The amendment effectively gave all male—but not female—citizens over the age of twenty-one the right to vote. Needless to say, pro-suffrage women were not happy—Mary included. The states eventually ratified the proposed amendment, but it drove a

Elizabeth Cady Stanton (*left*) and Susan B. Anthony (*right*) prioritized women's suffrage over universal suffrage rights. They believed that voting rights should be granted to white women before they were granted to Black men. Black women were largely left out of the conversation.

wedge between the supporters of the women's suffrage movement. Although Stanton and her allies in the movement had initially lobbied for universal suffrage, at their core they believed that white women should be given the vote before Black men. But Mary and others argued that the rights of white women should not be placed above those of Black Americans—that they were all in this fight together!

Stanton, Anthony, and other suffragists wanted a constitutional amendment giving women the right to vote. Mary angered them by arguing that there was no need for such an amendment because "We the People," as set forth in the US Constitution, included women as well as men. What's more, she pointed to the language of the first section of the Fourteenth Amendment, which recognized all persons born or naturalized in the United States as citizens. In a legal strategy that became known as the New Departure, she argued that since US-born women were citizens by birth and the Fourteenth Amendment said that citizens had the right to vote, she and other female citizens therefore had the right to vote. Using this argument, Mary tried to exercise her right to vote in Oswego, only to be turned away at the polls.

★ ★ ★

By the spring of 1866, Mary had moved to New York City. She loved the hustle and bustle of the city, but her reform dress still shocked many. One afternoon in June she went for a walk in Lower Manhattan, where her attire attracted quite a rowdy crowd. When she stepped into a hat shop on Canal Street, the rabble gathered around the shop windows, eager to see what Mary might be up to. The shop owner, concerned for Mary's safety, summoned two police officers to escort her home—against her wishes. But one of the officers had other ideas. He took her to the police station—roughly, she said—where he wanted to charge her for violating a city law forbidding women to appear in public wearing male attire. "I will have you broken," she told him.

The desk sergeant, who described her as "very defiant," asked whether she could read or write.

"I don't know a letter of the alphabet," she shot back sarcastically. Perhaps sensing that he had more than met his match, he declined to press charges and told the police officer to escort her through the crowd. "When I wish the protection of a policeman," she said, "I will ask an intelligent one."

A few days later, Mary was again arrested for disorderly conduct, wearing a "male costume," and attracting a crowd. This time they actually locked her up and set her bail at $300 (just over $5,000 in today's currency) to compel her "to keep the peace for a year." She spent several hours in jail until her lawyer could come and pay for her release.

Mary would not be intimidated. She filed a complaint of improper conduct against the first arresting officer, saying that he had arrested her for wearing masculine clothing and not for disturbing the peace. The complaint triggered a hearing before the police commission board, headed by Thomas Acton. Mary testified before a large crowd that she had worn this style of clothing for many years, including during several visits to New York City. She pointed out that fashionable female clothing, with its long, heavy skirts, picked up debris from city streets that

Women's clothing in the 1860s featured wide hoopskirts underneath long dresses. While the hoopskirt did keep the front hem off the ground, the backs of the dresses were usually longer and dragged on the ground.

were then often littered with horse manure and even raw human waste. Mary also stated that if a woman wanted to walk to the top of the hill to visit the Bunker Hill Monument, she risked having the wind blow up her hoopskirt, exposing her lower body.

"I wish it understood," she said, "that I wear this style of dress from the purest and the noblest principles and I believe that if there is anything a woman receives from Heaven, it is the right to protect herself morally and with the present style of dress there are circumstances where she cannot do it."

Elizabeth Miller, the owner of the hat shop, and her assistant also testified at the hearing. They stated that the crowd was not originally violent but that the officer himself had riled up the people. At one point during the testimony, Mary described her attempt to leave without the accompanying arresting officer: "While the officer fumbled in his pockets I showed my *Walker* powers and ran down stairs into the counting room, and told them of my adventure."

By the end of the hearing, the judge ordered the police to leave Mary alone, saying, "She's smart enough to take care of herself."

Mary's arrests and the hearing made the news. An editor at the *New York Times* wrote, "Her hat is the merest chip of straw. . . . Her dainty parasol, her bijoutry [jewelry], indeed everything but the ample pantaloons and coat terminating at the knees betokened the moderately fashionable woman." The reporter commended the desk sergeant for having a "small amount of common sense" when he declared the complaint against Mary trivial. The reporter also questioned whether the judge could "dictate what shall constitute in future a lady's street costume."

The *Brooklyn Daily Eagle* was more critical. Its reporter wrote that she was "entitled to every respect as a lady, and to respect for her opinions. As an abstract principle she has a right to dress as she pleases, provided she does not offend modesty." But the reporter pointed out that "there is a law on the Statute book which makes it a misdemeanor [a minor crime] for any person to appear in public dressed in the apparel of the opposite sex" and that the law "directs a policeman to arrest any person whose acts or conduct tends to collect a mob endangering the public peace. . . . The gathering of a mob of gaping idlers whenever Mrs. Walker appears on the street is a public annoyance, and it is a question whether the public should suffer for the gratification of personal eccentricity."

Two weeks after the hearing, Mary traveled to Syracuse to take part in a conference of the National Dress Reform Association. There she was elected president of the organization. Nearly eight hundred people heard her lecture, which included an account of her legal battles in New York City, her service in the Civil War, and her views on suffrage. She even included a little comic relief. There had been a heated public debate about the appropriate punishment for the former Confederate president, Jefferson Davis. She suggested that they should

The National Dress Reform Association was founded by James Caleb Jackson in 1857. Jackson was a physician who, like Mary and her father, believed that the corsets and heavy dresses of the 1800s were bad for women's health. He encouraged women to wear the Bloomer costume or reform dress.

dress him in a long hoopskirt and make him do the work of a woman managing a four-story home. Such punishment, she said, would be worse than anything else he could imagine. Her suggestion was greeted with laughter and applause.

★ ★ ★

In August 1866, Mary received an invitation from the National Association for the Promotion of Social Science to attend its meeting in Manchester, England, to be held October 8. The association sought to improve public health, labor relations, prisons, and women's education. She hoped her visit abroad would boost her name recognition and the public's respect for her work.

The invitation to the meeting did not include money for her expenses, and Mary couldn't afford to pay for her travel and lodging. Instead, Mary's friends pitched in the money she needed to make the trip. She set sail for Liverpool, England, in August on the ship *Caledonia*. This early departure would give her time to tour local hospitals and gain insight into the progress of women's rights in Great Britain.

Two of her traveling companions were Dr. Susannah Way Dodds and her Scottish husband, Andrew. Dodds, like Mary, was trained as an eclectic physician and was an advocate of dress reform and women's suffrage. While Mary enjoyed the company of a kindred spirit, the passage itself was difficult. Not only were the ocean waves rough, but she also had to endure being packed into close quarters with many smokers. "I have been sick enough to feel as disagreeable as possible," she wrote her family while on board the ship. She wished all tobacco would be dumped into the Atlantic Ocean—a sentiment she didn't hesitate to share with her fellow passengers. Indeed, later in life she became notorious for approaching any man she saw smoking and knocking the cigarette or cigar from his mouth with a tightly rolled umbrella. It wasn't just that the tobacco smoke bothered her, but she thought that smoking, along with consuming alcohol, was an unhealthy vice.

After the *Caledonia* landed in Liverpool, Mary and her two friends traveled to Scotland. She toured several hospitals, including the Glasgow Royal Infirmary. The head of its surgical department was Joseph Lister, the "father of modern surgery." Before Lister, most surgeons didn't bother to wash their hands or instruments in between treating patients. They even took pride in the blood stains on their aprons as a mark of experience. The germ theory of disease—the idea that microscopic organisms could cause disease—was in its infancy.

Lister suspected that germs caused disease and thought they could be killed by an antiseptic solution. He insisted that the surgeons he supervised wash their hands with antiseptic before and after operating on patients.

Joseph Lister began practicing medicine around the time when anesthetics became widely used in 1844. Anesthetics made surgeries painless for patients, and therefore, more physicians began to treat patients with surgery. However, these surgeries were often deadly before Lister recommended the use of antiseptics to keep doctors' hands and tools clean.

They cleaned their instruments and operating room with the same solution. During her visit, Mary was invited to attend any operations she chose to observe Lister's surgery routines.

Mary did a little sightseeing in Scotland before traveling to Manchester to attend the association meeting. The theme of the meeting was "Legislation on Social Subjects," and one of the first sessions Mary took part in was "The Repression of Crime." She weighed in on the death penalty, which she called barbaric and un-Christian. She also discussed infanticide—the murder of babies—which was not uncommon in the nineteenth century, especially among unmarried mothers. Echoing an article she had written for the *Sibyl* in 1859, she argued that public shaming and a lack of sympathy led many unmarried mothers to believe they had no choice but to kill their own infants. She urged compassion for women and their babies. The audience responded with wild applause.

Mary gave a lecture that she titled "Crinoline," focusing on the heavy clothing fashionable women wore and the damage it did to their bodies. In another session, she weighed in on suffrage for women, predicting that they would be able to vote within ten years.

Mary was a sensational hit in England. The *London Globe* called her a "prima donna assoluta," or absolute first lady—a term usually reserved for leading female opera singers. She was invited to social gatherings by people eager to hear her talk about her progressive ideas. On November 20, 1866, she spoke at St. James's Hall in London. The title of her lecture was "The Experiences of a Female Physician in College, Private Practice and in the Federal Army." As she looked out into the two-thousand-seat auditorium, she saw that all the seats were taken, with many attendees standing in the aisles.

The audience hushed when she stepped onto the stage wearing her dress reform outfit. But a group of male medical students seemed intent on disrupting her speech. When she said that some people had told her she should marry a doctor rather than become one, the rowdy med students shouted, "Hear, Hear!"

She told the audience that some people thought they shouldn't have to pay a woman doctor as much as a male doctor. "My education has cost me as much as that of my learned brothers has cost them," she said. "I have had far greater difficulties to overcome, and if any difference is to be made, it ought to be in favor of the female physician." As the medical students continued to interrupt her with insults and laughter, she sat down and waited until the police came and arrested them.

She described an incident in a DC hospital in which she encountered a young soldier dying of typhus. "He opened his sunken eyes," she recounted, "and in a pleading tone said, 'Let me kiss you—twice, *only* twice!' His eyes looked glazed, his emaciated face had a yellow hue, his lips were parched and full of blisters." As she hesitated, another young soldier said he knew the dying man. "'Let him kiss you,' the soldier urged her, 'his hours on earth are numbered, and he cannot see distinctly; he thinks [you are] his sister; it will comfort him in his last moments.'" Mary held her cheek to his lips and allowed him to kiss her. She bathed his face as he sank into a quiet slumber. He died the next morning.

Mary's lecture was widely covered in the press, and responses were predictable. Some conservative newspapers mocked her. Others were alarmed that a woman should dare to do what they saw as a man's job, arguing that it was "not womanly to saw off legs and arms, and to operate on the tibia [the larger shinbone]."

Progressive newspapers praised her. The *London Anglo-American Times* wrote, "Her strange adventures, thrilling experiences, important services and marvelous achievements exceed anything that modern romance or fiction has produced. . . . She has been one of the greatest benefactors of her sex and of the human race."

A reporter for the *National Reformer* stated that she had captivated the audience with her "intrepid integrity . . . lofty morality," her "melodious voice," and "spontaneous grace."

Following her St. James's Hall lecture, invitations poured in from all over the United Kingdom. What was to have been a six-week visit became a lecture tour that extended well into 1867. She delivered many lectures on women's rights and temperance—the effort to limit or outlaw the consumption and production of alcoholic beverages, something Mary very much supported. One of her most popular lectures, "Dr. Mary E. Walker, Her Capture by the Confederates, and Four Months' Detention as a Prisoner of War," included a dramatic account of her encounter with Champ Ferguson. Over the coming months, she honed her skills as a speaker and as a businesswoman, booking and promoting her own events and negotiating her speaking fees. She was so in demand that she had to turn down some speaking invitations.

In June, Mary traveled to Paris, France. She was especially excited to visit the Paris Exposition. Officially opened a few weeks earlier by Emperor Napoleon III and his wife, Empress Eugénie, the exposition highlighted the history of labor and culture in forty-two countries and was the most expensive and elaborate festival the world had ever seen.

The Paris Exposition of 1867 had over fifty thousand exhibitors and was estimated to have attracted around fifteen million visitors. It covered over 100 acres (40 ha) of the Champ de Mars in Paris.

Mary toured the large exhibit-filled park and the central hall, taking in the Japanese and Siamese (now Thai) pavilions. An Egyptian hall featured replicas of Egyptian statues and monuments. Ever intellectually curious, Mary would probably have been fascinated by an exhibit featuring more than 450 medically useful plants collected in Central Africa by a French explorer and scientist.

She took pride in award-winning exhibits displaying ambulances, surgical instruments, and hospital equipment developed during the Civil War. An exhibit on clothing that included an example of reform dress was a special highlight for her. But she lost her temper when she discovered an American exhibit showing photographs of Robert E. Lee and other Confederate generals. She tore down a card describing Lee in positive terms. Not surprisingly, security officers escorted her from the room.

Political tensions had been high between France and the United States, and when the emperor announced the prize-winning entries in the exhibition, a band played the national anthem for every winning entry—except "The Star-Spangled Banner." Mary was not pleased. To show her displeasure, when she attended the Americans' Fourth of July banquet at the nearby Grand Hotel, she wore a sash decorated with stars and stripes over her usual reform outfit. At what one American journalist, Moncure Conway, described as an otherwise dull affair, nearly three hundred prominent Americans watched as Mary walked up to the head table and offered a toast to "Our soldiers and sailors." Then she kissed the flag she wore before gliding to her seat. Conway observed that "Dr. Mary Walker did not wait for the dancing that followed and, when she left, received an ovation from the French crowd in the courtyard on account of the glorious independence of her trousers; nowise concealed but decorated by her patriotic sash." Although, he added, "The applause must have been for Dr. Mary Walker's independence; uglier dress was never worn."

Mary stayed in Paris for four weeks. She visited several hospitals, where she was received warmly. At the Hôtel-Dieu Hospital, the interns invited Mary to join them for breakfast. "There was a goodly gathering around the [table]," a correspondent for the medical publication the *Lancet* wrote. "Even a vice-professor of the Faculty had claimed the favor of a seat,

The Hôtel-Dieu Hospital is one of the oldest hospitals in France. Located along the Seine River in Paris, it was originally constructed around the year 651. When Mary visited, the building was being rebuilt after being demolished due to extensive fire damage from the 1700s.

and the greatest good humor and highest spirits enlivened the entertainment." The young men raised a toast to the delighted Mary. It must have been a welcome change from the verbal attacks of the British medical students.

Mary returned to London in August. Her final lecture abroad, at the National Temperance League Rooms, was titled "Farewell Lecture to the Ladies of London, on Ladies' Reform Dress." She had learned valuable lessons on how to leverage her public persona to advance her agenda.

MARY AND THE FLAG

Mary's devotion to the US flag was legendary. At a meeting in 1863, she recited a poem she had written about the flag. It was a parody of a popular poem written by Eliza Cook in 1840, which begins, "I love it, I love it; and who shall dare / To chide me for loving that old arm-chair?" Here is Mary's version:

I love it! I love it! Oh, who shall dare
To chide me for loving that flag so fair?
I treasured it long for the patriot's pride
And wept for the heroes who for it died.
'Tis bound by a thousand spells to my heart,
Nothing on earth can e'er us part.

Would you learn the spell? There is liberty there,
Making that flag the fairest of the fair.
Then chide me not if here I wave
That flag, redeemed by brothers brave,
For while I live that flag shall be
Waving over you and me.
When I am buried 'neath the ground,
Wrap that flag my corpse around,
Plant that flag above my grave,
There let it wave! Let it wave!

Mary had her photo taken wrapped in an American flag while she was in Washington, DC. She was extremely devoted to the United States and took pride in this symbol of the country she loved.

CHAPTER 6

TOURING THE UNITED STATES

MARY RETURNED TO THE UNITED STATES in September 1867. Not yet thirty-five years old, the doctor was eager to reenter the fray of the reform movements she cared so much about. She spent most of her time in Washington, DC, and New York City, both hotbeds of reform activism. But after her exciting year in Europe, she found that her stardom didn't shine quite as brightly at home. She had to work hard to regain the influence she once had in the women's rights movement, which had by then narrowed its focus on the right to vote.

Unlike many other female activists, Mary didn't have financial support from a husband or other family members. She had to make her own living, so she worked hard to reestablish her medical practice in Washington, DC. It wasn't easy; many middle-class and wealthy clients were put off by her radical dress and activism. That was fine with Mary. She had learned more about labor issues while in England, and she had always sympathized with the poor and working class. Some physicians looked down on their colleagues who treated the poor, seeing this as a sign that they weren't proficient doctors. Mary, on the other hand, welcomed these patients, even setting up evening office hours to accommodate her patients' work schedules. As she worked, Mary befriended a number of like-minded activist women, including Belva Lockwood. They would become lifelong friends. Like Mary, Lockwood was born in upstate New York, became a teacher while still in her teens, and was passionate about abolition, voting rights, and temperance. And like Mary, Lockwood had overcome gender discrimination to earn a degree and practice in her chosen profession. The widowed mother had moved to Washington, DC, eager to be in the thick of the "great political center—this seething pot"—and to earn

In addition to being a leader of the women's suffrage movement, Belva Lockwood was a leader in law. She was the first woman to be accepted to the bar for the US Supreme Court in 1879, which means she was allowed to act as a lawyer in front of the Supreme Court.

a law degree from the new National University School of Law (now the George Washington University Law School). It was one of the few law schools that would accept women.

Mary also renewed her acquaintance with the major leaders of the women's movement: Susan B. Anthony, Lucy Stone, and Elizabeth Cady Stanton. She had a cordial, but not close, relationship with Clara Barton, whom Mary had met and worked with in Fredericksburg during the Civil War. Surrounded by activists, Mary longed for the excitement she had known when she was on the lecture circuit in Europe. Soon she was making plans for a short lecture tour in the United States.

She put her medical practice on hold for three months and spoke to audiences in New York and Connecticut. She had a decent reception, but it was nothing like the packed halls she had spoken to in Europe. Mary quickly learned that her lecture on her experiences as a Civil War surgeon and prisoner of war was not as popular as it was in Europe; the pain of war was too fresh for Americans, who had experienced it firsthand. She began to think about expanding her repertoire and returned to her medical practice in DC, determined to develop new lectures.

In June 1868, Mary gave a lecture at the Union League Hall titled "Pure Love and Sacred Marriage." Her theme was the need for equality and mutual respect in marriage. "Some men love women as children love dolls," she said, "and treat them just as dolls are treated. They dress them in all the finery they are capable of doing—fit them to exhibit until their clothes become old, and the beautiful color of the face is gone, and the eyes contracted and dim, and then like dolls they are laid aside for neighbor's dolls, or for more beautiful dolls in the windows of false society's market." She condemned the laws that made it difficult for women to obtain a divorce—no doubt inspired by her own experiences.

In July of that year, the US Congress officially ratified the Fourteenth Amendment. It was a huge advance for Black men, but its gender-specific language was a blow to women's suffrage. That fall, many women made symbolic attempts to vote anyway. In Vineland, New Jersey, 172 women, including 4 Black women, carried their own ballot box to the polls when their ballots were rejected.

On January 21, 1869, shortly after Mary's divorce was finally granted, she attended a Universal Franchise Association (UFA) convention in Washington, DC. The aim was to talk about the best ways to secure women's social and civil rights, including the right to vote. Mary and her friend Dr. Ellen Beard Harman, a fellow eclectic physician, both dressed in reform outfits and attracted a lot of attention. Not all of it was positive; many suffragists did not want to be associated with a woman who did not look traditionally feminine.

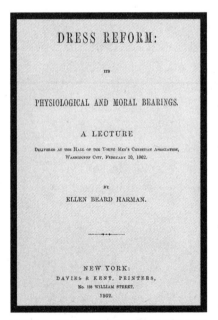

Like Mary, Ellen Beard Harman was a staunch supporter of dress reform. She published a lecture titled "Dress Reform: Its Physiological and Moral Bearings" in 1862, which outlined her reasons for wearing reform outfits.

When it was Mary's turn to speak, she proclaimed that she "had labored, suffered for the colored man, the white man and the women, but she was not willing to see another man made a voter until the whole female population of this country was enfranchised"—a statement that seemed at odds with her previous stance on suffrage for Black men and women as well as white women.

The audience agreed with Mary until she began describing how the law was used against women not just in terms of voting rights but in marriage rights as well.

She described the many ways in which the law had been used against her in her long battle to obtain a divorce. The audience began to hiss—they were progressive when it came to voting rights, but many were still conservative when it came to marriage and divorce. One man yelled, "We don't want to hear it!"

Mary replied, "Well, if you do not want to hear me, your daughter may suffer."

Lucretia Mott, who was presiding over the conference, attempted to silence her, but Mary gamely continued until she had finished. By that time, several people had left the hall, "so indecent was the language used by her in relating her grievances," one reporter wrote.

Racial disputes played a role in the conference. Clara Barton stated that she was willing to have Black men receive the right to vote first because she was sure "they would hold the door open wide for women." But Stanton spoke angrily about the fact that Black men would receive the right to vote before women.

Stanton and other like-minded activists put together a statement that read, "A *man's* government is worse than a *white* man's government, because, as you increase the number of tyrants, you made the condition of the disenfranchised class more hopeless and degraded."

This angered Dr. Charles Purvis, an influential Black man from Philadelphia, who said that the white women who championed their own rights above his were the "bitterest enemies of the negro." Mary was outraged. Perhaps unaware of her own privilege as a white person in the United States, she demanded an explanation of how white women had harmed Black Americans.

In the end, the convention's attendees adopted a much less controversial statement: "The privilege of casting a ballot is an individual right, not restricted by color or sex." Later, presumably after some behind-the-scenes negotiations, Purvis would publicly speak out in support of women's suffrage—an important step in repairing the fractured relationship between Black men and white women suffragists.

In February 1869, Congress passed the Fifteenth Amendment and sent it to the states for ratification. It strengthened the Fourteenth Amendment by explicitly prohibiting federal and state governments from denying citizens the right to vote based on "race, color, or previous condition of servitude." Once again, there was no mention of gender. Women were still denied the right to vote.

That spring, Mary and her friend Lydia Sayer Hasbrouck formed a national dress reform organization that aligned itself closely with the broader agenda of women's rights, including suffrage. The Mutual Dress Reform and Equal Rights Association held its first convention in New York City on April 28, with Mary serving as the organization's president. The first evening was not a success: a group of young men in the audience was so disruptive that the meeting had to be adjourned. Mary and Hasbrouck put their heads together that night and discussed a new

Lydia Sayer Hasbrouck was the founder and editor of the *Sibyl*, the women's rights periodical that frequently published Mary's writing. Like Mary, Hasbrouck was an eclectic physician, specializing in water therapy.

strategy to win over the audience. The next evening, Mary pulled a human skeleton that had seen better days—one of its limbs was missing—onto the stage. Amid raucous laughter, she struggled to arrange it in an upright position. At first, she thought the audience was laughing at her—after all, she had been the butt of many jokes—but when she realized they were laughing at the skeleton she joined in, saying this was "what many women would be like soon if they don't reform their dress." The skeleton was calculated to lighten things up, but it played a more serious role in her lecture because she used it to make "some remarkable observations on the hygienic, anatomical, and physiological aspects of the question of dress reform," as one reporter wrote in a positive account of her lecture.

Over the next few months, Mary applied for several federal government jobs—in the State Department, the Postal Service, and the Treasury Department. She thought that her service in the war would have earned her some sort of appointment, but time after time she was turned down. Her difficulties in finding a job led Mary to think more deeply about working women. By this time, nearly 15 percent of US women worked outside the home. Almost all of them were household servants or worked in factories. Mary wanted to convince these women that the fight for the right to vote was more important for them than for the middle-class women leading the suffrage movement. She didn't succeed in organizing a working women's movement for suffrage, but she never lost sight of their needs for medical care and education.

Without any luck in the job market, in September 1869, Mary embarked upon a nine-monthlong lecture tour that would take her to Ohio, Missouri, Kansas, Louisiana, Mississippi, and Texas. Although she sometimes shared the stage with other leading suffragists, including Anthony, Stanton, and Stone, she handled her own scheduling and booking. Her first stop, in Cincinnati, Ohio, did not get off to a promising start. On September 15, she joined suffragists from around the country at a meeting of the Ohio State Women's Suffrage Society. The organizers did not want her to speak because they didn't want dress reform to be associated with women's suffrage. A local reporter wrote that Mary was "the thorn in the flesh of the manager of the Convention. She was constantly anxious to be seen and heard, and the curiosity-hunting audience making calls for her." But members of the audience—and some of the delegates to the convention—wanted to hear what Mary had to say. The organizers backed down and gave her speaking slots both days of the meeting.

Mary was received even more poorly in October, when she traveled to St. Louis to attend the Missouri Woman's Suffrage Association meeting. Although Anthony and Stanton were among the invited speakers, Mary was not allowed on the stage. As usual, the press reported on her "pantaloons" with derision and repeated a false rumor that she advocated a law requiring all men to marry before the age of forty.

Mary spent most of October in Missouri, in Fulton and Kansas City, where she attracted respectable crowds. She crossed the Missouri River to Kansas and then traveled to towns across the state. Her lectures were usually about suffrage and dress reform, but she also spoke about fairness in law and on health and medical issues. The United States could not be a nation of freedom and democracy, she told her audiences, when women were denied the right to vote. Women who committed crimes, she pointed out, were tried under man-made laws with all-male juries. Men and women who opposed women's suffrage, she said, had seen little of the world and didn't understand the lives of working women. She also stated that women leading the temperance movement could help change laws if they could vote. That year—1869—was the year that a young wife and mother named Carrie Nation lost her husband, who died of alcoholism. Nation would become famous (and, to some, infamous) for her anti-alcohol activism, which included destroying saloons with her hatchet.

In Kansas City, Kansas, a police officer hauled Mary into jail for wearing masculine clothing. The judge quickly dismissed the case, and at least one local reporter sided with her: "As it is about the only sensible dress sensible women have adopted in this senseless age, we cannot understand why it is sensible men deride it."

Mary was in Leavenworth, Kansas, in mid-December when she received an interesting letter from Mary L. Reed of Port Gibson, Mississippi. A group of women in the city, the letter stated, wanted to form a "sisterhood" to promote women's rights. Would Mary come talk to the group and the public at large? They had already raised $450 and promised to pay her $600—the equivalent of $12,000 in modern money. Mary was intrigued. Not only was this a handsome fee, but the South was even more conservative than the rest of the country. Mary was eager to spread her message in a region that had not previously been open to women's suffrage and equal rights. Most suffragists did not even bother booking lecture tours in southern states. Mary canceled several bookings and wrote to Reed, saying that she could be in Mississippi by December 28. "My heart is filled with more than regard for the Southern Sisterhood," she wrote, "for you, like us, must feel the degradation of all unenfranchised women, in a professed to be, Republican country."

CARRIE NATION, THE TEMPERANCE MOVEMENT, AND PROHIBITION

In the early nineteenth century, many Americans had a serious drinking problem. By 1830 the average American over the age of fifteen drank almost 7 gallons (26 L) of alcohol every year—three times as much as Americans drink in the twenty-first century. Alcohol was considered a healthier substitute for water, which might be contaminated with disease-causing microbes. But alcohol abuse wreaked havoc on the lives of thousands of people. Women, who had few legal rights and were dependent on their husbands for support, were among the most vulnerable to the social consequences of alcohol addiction, which often led to unemployment, poverty, and domestic violence.

And so the temperance movement was born, primarily led by women and rooted in Protestant churches. Other reformers, including abolitionists and suffragists, also embraced it. At first, the temperance movement urged moderation in drinking, although activists ultimately demanded that government prohibit alcohol altogether.

Carrie Nation was one of the many people who campaigned against alcohol consumption. However, her violent methods were not always accepted by other temperance supporters.

Carrie Nation's furious anti-alcohol campaign came from personal experience. When she was twenty-one years old, she married a man who had served as a doctor in the Union army. But he was haunted by the horrors of war. He drank heavily to try to forget the lives he couldn't save. He showed up drunk to their wedding and stayed that way, more or less, until he died of alcohol-related causes sixteen months later. Carrie was left with an infant daughter and a fierce hatred of alcohol.

A few years later, she married David Nation, who was a preacher and lawyer. They settled in Kansas, and she became involved in the newly formed Woman's Christian Temperance Union (WCTU). Nation felt that the WCTU wasn't doing enough to stop the sale and consumption of alcohol. She went on a nationwide campaign, storming saloons and expounding on the evils of liquor while bashing the places to pieces with a hatchet in one hand and a Bible in the other. She staged protests on the Capitol lawn and demanded that presidents stop serving wine at official functions. She sold brooches and pins shaped like hatchets to fund her activism. She began spelling her name "Carry," the way her father once spelled it, so that she could say she was there to "Carry A. Nation" to prohibition—a nationwide ban on alcohol.

Nation collapsed onstage during a speech in 1911 and died soon after. Her final words were "I have done what I could." The Eighteenth Amendment, which prohibited the manufacture and sale of alcohol in the United States, was ratified nine years later. It was difficult to enforce, however, and it led to the illegal production and sale of liquor and a rise in organized crime and violence. The amendment was repealed in 1933.

Mary paid her own way to Port Gibson, only to find that there was no Mary L. Reed to greet her, no Southern Sisterhood, and no $600. The letter was a cruel hoax, intended to demean her and the women's movement. The local paper reported that Mary gave a speech anyway, although it did not give any details about the substance of her talk. Instead, the reporter wrote that "the *cause* of the lecture [was] an insatiable thirst for notoriety, and a shrew's determination to be heard." The reporter did have the decency to scold the people who carried out the hoax, writing, "There is and can be no excuse for so scurvy a trick, and it should be condemned, as it should be, by this entire community."

Mary decided to make the best of a bad thing. She visited Vicksburg and Jackson, Mississippi, drawing disappointingly small crowds. Then she traveled across Louisiana from late January 1870 through early March, lecturing to sparse crowds and receiving mostly negative press coverage. In Clinton, Louisiana, she gave a lecture that was pretty well attended, so she scheduled another one for the following night. The local paper urged its readers to stay away from the second lecture because Mary had been seen strolling companionably with a Black woman.

In early February, Captain Thomas P. Jenks offered Mary a buggy ride from Clinton to Bayou Sara on her way to New Orleans. She gladly accepted, but late that afternoon, armed bandits forced them to stop and throw all their money on the ground. Mary turned over sixty hard-earned dollars. She was so frustrated that she held a ten cent piece between her fingers and sarcastically asked if they wanted that too. Her comment led the robbers to rifle through their trunks, threatening a body search and murder if they found any more money. Luckily, the travelers were spared and continued on their journey.

The robbery made national news. Predictably, some newspapers found Mary partly to blame. One Pennsylvania reporter wrote that if she "will persist in dressing like a man, she must expect to be mistaken for a man, and sometimes enjoy the inalienable right of being robbed like any other man."

Mary stayed in New Orleans for a couple of months. The Fifteenth Amendment had just been ratified. People had suffrage on their minds. Women suffragists hoped that since the amendment didn't mention gender, they might be permitted to vote. (They were not.) Mary gave several lectures in the city, including one titled "Men's Rights, Women's Wrongs, and Women's Suffrage."

During her stay, Mary learned that a young woman in Algiers, a neighborhood in New Orleans, had been charged with killing her baby. She immediately went to the woman's aid and worked with her lawyer to get the woman acquitted. The young woman was eventually found not guilty but not before being subjected to a trial presided over by a male judge and an all-male jury, who heard the most intimate details of her life. This, Mary believed, was a prime example of why women needed to have a voice in shaping legislation and the judicial system. "A woman has been tried today," Mary wrote in a letter to the editor of the *New Orleans Republican*, "but not by a woman judge, not by a woman attorney, not by a woman jury, but all the officials were men. . . . What about people being tried by their peers? The woman will be acquitted because there is no evidence to convict her, but the principle is the same."

The local police arrested Mary twice for wearing her reform clothing, but the charges were dismissed both times. Mary complained to George L. Cain, the police superintendent. He was not sympathetic, saying that he was not even sure if she was really a woman.

Mary's gender was questioned multiple times in her life. Her shortened skirts may have looked similar to the long suit coats men wore at the time. Mary never claimed to be a man; she simply demanded the respect afforded to the men of her time.

Mary wrote another letter to the editor of the *New Orleans Republican* describing her treatment in the city. The paper sent a reporter to interview Mary, who was more than happy to share her thoughts on dress reform and women's rights. He asked her about a groundbreaking trial that had just taken place in Wyoming Territory (which was not yet a state but still followed US law). There, women had served on a grand jury (a body that examines accusations of crimes and decides if formal charges are warranted) for the first time in the history of the United States. The previous fall, the territory had also granted women the right to vote. This happened in part because leaders wanted to attract more women to the territory, where the ratio of men to women was six to one, and because of the racist reasoning that if Black and Chinese men (many of whom worked building railroads in the American West) had the right to vote, then women—especially white women—should enjoy the same right. As a result of their newly granted right to vote, women were eligible to sit on juries. The reporter wanted to know what Mary thought of this controversial new development.

"I am proud of these noble women jurors," Mary told him, "who have been honored with the first duties of the kind in this great republic (beg your pardon—*half republic*)." Mary could not resist mentioning that most women still could not vote in this country, or republic:

> *As to women and men being locked up all together*
> *to talk over cases of justice and injustice, life and*
> *death, I fail to see why it is not as respectable as it*
> *is to be locked up in a suit of dressing and danc-*
> *ing rooms, where women wear low bodied dresses,*
> *short sleeves, and all other absurdities of fashionable*

I Could Not Do Otherwise

helplessness. . . . It is perfectly disgusting to see the
ideas of sex dragged into everything, where sex has
nothing whatever to do with the case.

The reporter complimented Mary on her style of dress, saying that "society would be the gainer if all women would dress sensibly."

Mary responded with good humor, "You are right; I am glad of the opportunity of telling a man he has arrived at correct conclusions."

Mary also acknowledged the difficulties of challenging society's norms. "All people are not heroes in all things," she told the reporter. Then, in what was surely a reference to herself, she added, "Women, as well as men, who can endure to be misunderstood for a great length of time, are few indeed, and those alone who feel the importance of a great principle and the certainty of its ultimate triumph."

The sympathetic and fair interview in the *New Orleans Republican* was the exception, not the norm, during Mary's suffrage tour. Mary and other touring suffragists were often subjected to ridicule in the press. At one lecture, a young man in the audience interrupted her, shouting, "Are you the Mary that had a little lamb?"

"No," she responded, "but your mother had a little jackass!" This exchange was written up and reprinted in papers across the country.

Instead of calling out the man's rude comment, the reporter used the anecdote as an example of Mary's "unfeminine" behavior.

The *New Orleans Times-Picayune* reprinted a sarcastic poem that Albert, her ex-husband, sent to the *Independence* (Missouri) *Sentinel*:

The bird calls from his golden cage
Its mate far in the wild wood;
And so my soul still wails for thee,
Bright angel of my childhood.

But if our fate, a cruel lot,
Hath cut our hearts assever,
Why, Mary, bring my trousers back,
And then go vote forever.

Mary was long past caring what Albert thought of her, but she craved public approval. She claimed indifference to the near-constant barrage of abuse from the newspapers, but the insults probably took a heavy toll on her psyche.

After a brief tour in Texas, Mary returned to Washington, DC, where she gave several lectures before going to her hometown of Oswego for the summer. There, the audiences were more receptive to her lectures about women's suffrage. She spent her time traveling between DC and New York City for the rest of the year, giving a variety of speeches on reform topics. Her reform dress continued to attract attention; at one point, dozens of angry men and boys followed her down the street throwing bricks, oyster shells, sardine boxes, and wads of wet paper at her. Undeterred, Mary kept walking.

CHAPTER 7

AUTHOR AND ACTIVIST

IN THE SPRING OF 1871, MARY published a book based on the many lectures she had given over the years. She titled it *Hit*, referencing the many verbal assaults that she and other dress reform advocates had endured. Mary wasn't afraid to hit back.

The opening page featured a full-length portrait of Mary wearing her reform outfit. She dedicated the book to her parents, dress reformers, women physicians, and that "Great Sisterhood, which embraces women with their thousand unwritten trials and sorrows . . . in the hope that it will . . . place in your hands that power which shall emancipate you from the bondage of all that is oppressive."

Mary's portrait showcases the shortened curly hairstyle she favored later in her life. Her Medal of Honor is pinned to her reform outfit over her heart.

The theme of the book was women's equality, especially in the context of marriage, and its eight chapters dealt with love and marriage, dress reform, tobacco, temperance, women's suffrage, divorce, labor, and religion. Mary wrote that some states allowed girls as young as twelve and boys as young as fourteen to marry and said that "such *children Marriages* will not be suffered, when women are enfranchised, and have a voice in making the laws." She argued that a married woman should be encouraged to keep her own name, which is "as dear to her as a man's is to him."

In her chapter on dress reform, Mary used her medical background to argue that the uncomfortable fashionable dresses of the day contributed to unhappiness in a marriage. She wrote, "Let a horse be compelled to wear a harness that is uncomfortable, and with all his great strength of nerves, but a little time will elapse before he is so restless that his driver feels obliged to seek out and remedy the irritating cause. But if a human being writhes under something that injures the nervous system, others are not as careful as they should be, to ascertain the *cause*, and hence the censure under which many poor wives labor."

Mary used the horse analogy several times in her dress reform chapter, perhaps believing that since many people understood the need to keep their horses—then the primary mode of transportation—happy and comfortable, they might apply that same understanding to the treatment of women.

She considered tobacco and alcohol not just unhealthy but evil and wrote that they were responsible for wrecking otherwise happy marriages. At the time, some physicians prescribed tobacco for various ailments, to which Mary responded, "Such a one ought to be sent to a lunatic asylum, for the purpose of having the smoke extracted from his brain, to make room for more knowledge of materia-medica [remedies]."

Mary also advocated for better working conditions and appreciation for laboring men and women. She predicted that in the future, "the people of the day will charge the great land-owners, and stock-owners, and *great everybodies*, with self-ishness unparalleled, when they read that many fathers never saw any of their children by day-light, except on Sunday, as they were all day at work in factories, mines and railroads."

Mary knew that the chapter on divorce would be the most controversial. "No one can believe more firmly than the writer in the sacredness of the marriage relation," she wrote, but she stated that too many marriages are the joining of "purity and impurity" or a faithful and unfaithful partner. These, she argued, are not true marriages.

Although she did not mention her own terrible marriage and divorce, she summed it up when she concluded, "To be deprived of a Divorce is like being shut up in a prison because some one attempted to kill you. The wicked one takes his ease and continues his *course*, and you take the slanders, without the power to defend yourself."

Hit wasn't a best seller, and Mary didn't make a great deal of money from the book, but it was widely read by suffragists in the United States and Europe.

Writing *Hit* did not consume all of Mary's time that year. In April, Mary and Belva Lockwood led a group of suffragists, including Frederick Douglass, to present the office that oversaw voter registration in Washington, DC, with a petition for female voter registration. They hoped to sign up to vote then and there, and each woman carried a bouquet of flowers for the "gallant clerk who should register her." Mary gave a short speech while the women filled out their forms, saying, "These women have assembled to exercise the right of citizens of a professed-to-be republican country, and if you debar them of the right to register, you but add new proof that this is a tyrannical government, sustained by force and not by justice." The registrar took the women's completed forms but did not record them.

Two years earlier, Mary had met a woman named Victoria Woodhull and her sister, Tennie Claflin. The sisters were spiritualists, believing that the spirits of the dead could communicate with the living, and had set up a practice as mediums, or psychics. In a lucky break, they became spiritual advisers to Cornelius Vanderbilt, a fabulously wealthy railroad magnate whose wife had recently died. Not only did they supposedly help Vanderbilt contact his dead wife, but they passed on stock trading tips from the spirit world that earned him millions of dollars. The elderly Vanderbilt was so smitten with the sisters, especially Tennie, that he helped them set up their own stock brokerage firm in New York City—the first ever brokerage firm owned by women. They used the fortune they made from their brokerage firm to start a newspaper, the *Woodhull & Clafin's Weekly*, which promoted women's suffrage, divorce and labor reform, and spiritualism. The sisters also promoted free love.

The two radical reformers, Mary and Woodhull, immediately clicked. Like Mary, Woodhull believed that the Constitution already gave women, as citizens, the right to vote. They both believed that women should continue to try to exercise their voting rights and that their actions would lead to laws specifically giving women the right to vote. There was no need, they argued, for a constitutional amendment. Also like Mary, Woodhull was a controversial figure in the women's suffrage movement, in part because she considered the right to divorce essential to women's equality.

In January 1872, Mary joined Woodhull, Belva Lockwood, Elizabeth Cady Stanton, and other leading suffragists as delegates to the national convention of the National Woman Suffrage Association (NWSA) in Washington, DC. The association was not yet ready to accept all Woodhull's ideas—she called for a revolution to change the Constitution—but it allowed her to speak anyway. In the summer of 1871, Woodhull had used her newspaper as a platform to announce her candidacy for the president of the United States—the first woman ever to do so. She named Frederick Douglass as her running mate—seemingly without consulting him. Although she knew that no woman stood much chance of winning, Mary established the Victoria League to support Woodhull's candidacy in the 1872 presidential election.

Victoria Woodhull announced her candidacy for president under the Cosmo-Political Party. The party was renamed the Equal Rights Party in 1872.

While Woodhull and Mary were good friends and allies, the strained relationship between Stanton and Mary was evident as it became clear that Mary would not be asked to be a speaker at the NWSA convention. The audience began to chant, "Dr. Mary Walker—Dr. Walker!—Walker!"

Stanton stepped up to the stage, saying, "Walker is not on the platform, at least not on the programme of speakers. As we pay for the hall we have the right to say who shall speak."

The convention ended without Mary being allowed to speak—evidence of the growing rift between Mary and her supporters, including Lockwood and Woodhull, and other leaders in the women's suffrage movement.

Though the war had ended years before, Mary renewed her efforts to make sure that Civil War nurses were given pensions. She wrote to women she knew who had served as nurses in the military, asking them for details about their service and whether they knew of any other women who had served during the war. On January 24, 1872, Massachusetts congressman Benjamin F. Butler, a former general in the Union army and staunch supporter of women's rights, introduced a bill on behalf of Mary and the "women who labored for the sick and wounded, during the late war" to the House of Representatives. The bill asked that women who served for ninety days or more be granted the "same bounties, the same grants of land, and the same pensions, that the United States is giving the men who served the Government as soldiers." A second section of the bill requested that women who served in the war be granted the right to vote. Eventually, the first section of the bill, but not the second, was passed. The women would be granted $20 monthly pensions—about $466 in twenty-first-century money—only slightly lower than that paid to male soldiers who had been injured in the war. It was one of Mary's proudest achievements.

On that same day, Mary and Belva Lockwood, along with a crowd of supporters, went before the House Judiciary

Mary was not included in this portrait collection titled "Representative Women" from 1870. Clockwise from the top are images of Lucretia Mott, Elizabeth Cady Stanton, Mary Livermore, Lydia Maria Francis Child, Susan B. Anthony, and Sara Jane Lippincott. The central portrait depicts Anna Elizabeth Dickinson. These women were some of the most popular on the lecture circuit who spoke about suffrage, temperance, abolition, and education reform.

Committee to present a petition for women's suffrage that had been signed by thirty-five thousand women from across the United States. Lockwood gave a speech before presenting the petition to Representative Butler, who presented it to the Congress. Years later, when Stanton, Anthony, and other prominent suffragists published their *History of Woman Suffrage*, they heaped praise on the document and Lockwood's efforts. Mary, who by that time had found herself completely ostracized by the mainstream suffrage movement, was not mentioned.

When the 1872 presidential election arrived, Mary, along with hundreds of other women across the country, marched to the polls in an attempt to vote, some of them singing, "We are coming, Uncle Sam, with fifteen million more." Most, including Mary, were turned away at the polls, but Susan B. Anthony somehow managed to cast her ballot for Ulysses S. Grant, who, while no great champion of women, was a better option than the Democratic nominee Horace Greeley, who was outspokenly opposed to women's suffrage. Anthony's daring feat became national news. A few weeks later, Anthony was arrested and charged with illegal voting. She was freed on bail and spent the coming months lecturing about her case, hoping to sway public opinion.

Anthony's trial was held in June 1873. She was found guilty by an all-male jury and fined $100, the equivalent of about $2,300 today. She refused to pay "a dollar of your unjust penalty."

On January 15, 1873, Mary presented to Congress a pamphlet titled *Crowning Constitutional Argument*. Addressed to lawmakers, the pamphlet summed up Mary's argument that the Constitution already included women's right to vote, since they were citizens. She felt that to support another amendment specifically granting women the vote would deny that women had ever been citizens. Mary believed that Congress needed to pass a law clarifying women's voting rights. She concluded with a call encouraging women to vote: "And now, my sisters, *lose no time* in your exercise of the 'rights, privileges and amenities' guaranteed to you, since the *protection of such rights* is guaranteed as well."

Mary's presentation to Congress took place the day before the National Woman Suffrage Association's annual national convention. The timing was surely not a coincidence. Anthony and Stanton resented all the attention Mary's pamphlet was getting, and her argument undermined their desire for a constitutional amendment, which increasingly appeared to be the only way women would get the vote.

Mary attended the conference and sat quietly onstage the first day of the convention, although she was not called upon to speak. One reporter observed, "There seems to be a disposition of the women composing this convention to ignore Dr. Mary Walker . . . and some of them expressed regret that she should make herself so conspicuous."

The second day, Mary took matters into her own hands. Without waiting for an introduction or invitation to speak, she stepped up to the podium. Anthony hastily introduced her, and Mary launched into a speech about the leadership of the NWSA. She described her work for the movement in the United States and abroad and claimed that she was being shunned because of her international fame. Instead of praising Anthony for casting a ballot in the presidential election, she chided her for swearing to be a male citizen in order to vote (Anthony later disputed this). She believed women should proudly vote as women. Mary admonished NWSA leaders for abandoning dress reform and criticized them for not supporting the racial civil rights outlined in the Fourteenth and Fifteenth Amendments.

Mary's speech was greeted with both applause and derision. "As much as I have done for the cause of woman suffrage," she told them, "I shall continue to work in the same direction—even for you who hissed, for you need it more than anyone else."

In March, Stanton wrote to a friend, "I suppose as I sat there I looked patient & submissive but I could have boxed that Mary Walkers ears with a vengeance." Her anger was no doubt made worse by the fact that Mary's *Crowning Constitutional Argument* was a direct rebuttal of Stanton's support of a constitutional amendment giving women the right to vote.

Mary's *Crowning Constitutional Argument* received widespread national coverage. She would print revised versions at least eight times, but she maintained her core argument.

That spring, Mary decided once again to try to get a job with the federal government. She applied for a clerkship within the Treasury Department. She knew Treasurer Francis Spinner and knew that he had hired women during the Civil War. She reasoned that she could work for the Treasury during the day and see patients and write in the evening. When she got no reply, she went directly to President Grant's office, but he refused to see her. She returned, day after day, only to be turned away.

Still, Mary knew how to get someone's attention. She bought a little gas stove and set up camp in the corridor outside the East Room of the president's Executive Mansion. In Mary's time, people considered the White House to be the property of the citizens. She just took the idea a little further than most. A lot further.

President Grant finally gave in and agreed to meet with her. A journalist for the *Washington Chronicle* wrote, "Grant has since that trying time been frequently heard to say that the campaign before Richmond, on the James, was nothing to the manner in which Dr. Mary . . . issued proclamations announcing that she intended to fight it out . . . if it took all summer. Grant at last surrendered."

President Grant promised her work if Mary would promise never to camp out in the building again. Mary agreed, and then he told her that she would have to wear traditional women's clothing in her workplace. Mary accepted the clerkship—a decent-paying job with a $1,200 annual salary (about $28,000 in today's currency)—and showed up to work in her usual reform dress. The doorkeepers at the Treasury Building turned her away. She kept reporting to work almost every day for more than a year but was never allowed in. As she still needed the income, she filed a petition with Congress seeking $900 in back pay. She had faithfully showed up to work; it was not her fault that they wouldn't let her do her job. Members of Congress agreed with her, and she was eventually paid.

In 1874 Mary began receiving a small pension of $8.50 a month (worth about $207 today) for the damage to her eyes she had suffered at Castle Thunder Prison. Mary also tirelessly pushed Congress to grant her a pension for her work in the army. It would take a long time. It wasn't until 1890, at the age of sixty-six, that Mary was awarded an additional $20 a month—the same amount allocated to the female nurses.

Mary decided to skip the 1874 NWSA convention, but she couldn't stay away from the action for long. She returned in January 1875. The event did not go well for her. Although she had not been invited to speak the first day, Mary took to the podium after the first speech of the evening, asking Elizabeth Cady Stanton to recognize and introduce her. Stanton reminded Mary that she was not scheduled to speak until the next evening. Knowing full well that Mary preferred the honorific Dr. Walker, Stanton asked the audience if "Mrs. Walker" should be allowed to speak this evening.

"That's not my name," Mary objected. The audience hissed and booed as Mary tried to speak, until Susan B. Anthony stepped in.

"We all believe in the freedom of speech," Anthony said, "but we foot the bills and want to do this to suit ourselves." Mary shot back, "Yes, she foots the bills and asks you people to pay for it."

When Mary was finally allowed to take the podium the following evening, she told the audience that she was hurt by the way the leaders of the NWSA had tried to erase her contributions to the suffrage movement. Anthony interrupted her, asking the audience if they wanted to listen to Mary's personal complaints. As the crowd responded, "No, no," Mary told Anthony to stop dictating to her. "If the truth is a tirade, all right," she said.

Mary continued speaking, focusing on suffrage and dress reform. Stanton shot down her request for a resolution requesting Congress to pass a law defining appropriate clothing for women, which would include reform dress. Stanton was happy with the status quo as far as women's fashion; she felt that Mary's obsession with dress reform distracted from the cause of women's suffrage. But when Anthony adjourned the meeting for a lunch break, Mary remained on the stage, where she read her *Crowning Constitutional Argument*, noting that it had been omitted from the 1873 convention's report. Most of the audience stayed to listen, rewarding her with applause. Although Mary was usually a gifted speaker, she stumbled over a few words. She apologized, saying that she was not as young as she used to be (she was by then forty-two years old) and had difficulty with her eyesight.

The rift between Mary and leaders of the women's suffrage movement, especially Stanton and Anthony, never healed. While Mary continued to support women's suffrage, she began to focus more on dress reform, tying it to issues relating to women's bodies and sexual health.

Mary headed west in the fall of 1875 to give a series of lectures. Her first stops were in Ogden and Salt Lake City, Utah, where she spoke about dress reform. She delivered her speech to a packed house in Ogden, and many people had to be turned away at the door. She continued her tour west to California. In January 1876, she gave a new lecture titled "Pure Love and Sacred Marriage" to an all-woman audience. The next night, she spoke to an all-male audience on "Woman." These gender-specific lectures were prototypes that Mary was developing into a new book for men on sexuality, sexual relations, and male promiscuity—topics that were not considered suitable for a mixed audience.

When the inevitable criticism of her subject matter arose, one of her defenders was Julia Ward Howe, the poet who wrote the lyrics to "The Battle Hymn of the Republic" in 1861. Howe was not as conservative on matters of sexuality as most women of the time and had even written some fairly erotic poems. Mary was "a good, true woman," Howe wrote in the *Atlanta Constitution*. Howe was much admired in the public eye, and her endorsement was especially valuable to Mary.

CRIMES OF FASHION
Cross-Dressing and the Law

In Mary's time, laws regarding cross-dressing were meant to reinforce gender norms: women were expected to dress and act a certain way, and men, another. Violating those norms was seen as a threat to the fabric of society. An 1845 New York law that was used to prosecute women for cross-dressing stemmed from a statute that stated, "Every person who, having his face painted, discolored, covered or concealed, or being otherwise disguised, in a manner calculated to prevent him from being identified, shall appear in any road or public highway, or in any field, lot, wood or inclosure, may be pursued and arrested."

Over time, the law was interpreted as applying to women who dressed as men, on the grounds that they were in disguise. Other states and cities soon adopted more explicit anti-cross-dressing laws. A San Diego law prohibited people from "appearing in a public place, or in a place open to public view, in apparel customarily worn by the opposite sex, with the intent to deceive another person of committing an illegal act." Cross-dressing people were commonly believed to be prostitutes at the time. The law, which was repealed only in 1996, was used to discriminate against transgender people.

Over time, thanks to people like Mary, it became more acceptable for women to wear trousers and other so-called masculine attire. Public acceptance of men wearing clothing traditionally reserved for women has been slower in coming. And although there are no longer laws of this kind on the books, transgender people—especially women of color—are routinely harassed by the police on suspicion of prostitution, which has come to be known as "walking while trans."

Mary returned to the East Coast that spring. She headed directly to Philadelphia, where the Centennial Exhibition of 1876, the first official World's Fair to be held in the United States, was set to open in May. She may have helped set up displays on clothing and medicine in the Women's Pavilion. The organizers of the Women's Centennial Executive Committee, led by Elizabeth Duane Gillespie, decided not to include exhibits on suffrage and women's rights in the pavilion. This angered Susan B. Anthony, and so on July 4, as the Declaration of Independence was read in Independence Hall (the site where the Second Continental Congress signed the Declaration of Independence), Anthony marched onto the stage. She presented the speaker with the Declaration of Rights of the Women of the United States while her fellow suffragists distributed copies to the crowd. Outside the hall, she read the declaration, which concluded,

And now, at the close of a hundred years, as the hour-hand of the great clock that marks the centuries points to 1876, we declare our faith in the principles of self-government; our full equality with man in natural rights; that woman was made first for her own happiness, with the absolute right to herself—to all the opportunities and advantages life affords for her complete development; and we deny that dogma of the centuries, incorporated in the codes of all nations—that woman was made for man—her best interests, in all cases, to be sacrificed to his will. We ask of our rulers, at this hour, no special favors, no special privileges, no special legislation. We ask justice, we ask equality, we ask that all the civil and political rights that belong to citizens of the United States, be guaranteed to us and our daughters forever.

The press, meanwhile, continued to mock and belittle Mary. In September a reporter for the *New York Times* wrote, "The other day that curious anthropoid, Miss Dr. Mary Walker, was bitten by an injudicious dog. The thoughtless person, on hearing of this incident, will, of course, feel some natural pity for the dog." Claiming that "the female skirt is a complete barrier to the attacks of hungry dogs," the reporter wrote that if dress reformers insisted on wearing pants, they should be made of sheet iron. "As for Doctor Walker, she will probably be satisfied with nothing less than copper trousers, securely riveted, and polished more brightly than the capstan of a man-of-war," the reporter jeered.

DECLARATION AND PROTEST
OF THE
WOMEN OF THE UNITED STATES
BY THE
NATIONAL WOMAN SUFFRAGE ASSOCIATION,
JULY 4th, 1876.

The Declaration of Rights of the Women of the United States was known by multiple titles when it was first published. In this publication, it was titled "Declaration and Protest of the Women of the United States."

★ ★ ★

By the time the next NWSA annual convention rolled around in January 1877, suffragists were feeling weary. They had been fighting for women's right to vote for years, with no end in sight. The old guard—Anthony, Stanton, and others—often clashed with younger newcomers to the movement, referring to them as "babies" who failed to respect the decades of work they had put into the movement.

Mary, as usual, opposed a constitutional amendment, saying that "she wanted her rights restored, not an amendment to give her a right that she already has." She caused a commotion when she interrupted the speech of Phoebe Couzins, a suffragist and lawyer from St. Louis, Missouri, to deliver her argument opposing the amendment.

Half of the audience called out "Couzins," with the other half shouting "Mary!" Fed up with the commotion, Anthony called the police to restore order and arrest Mary. Before she could be arrested, Mary took her seat.

The incident stung. It was one thing to have city cops arrest Mary on the streets. It was quite another to have her sister suffragists call for her arrest. Mary told Anthony and Stanton, "You are not working for the cause, but for yourselves."

In March of that year, Mary found herself at the center of yet another controversy. Wearing her usual reform dress, she tried to enter the Treasury Building to see the secretary of the treasury. She wanted to talk to him about the position she had been given by President Grant. The building's doorkeeper, Walter R. Baker, ordered her to leave the building. Mary objected but gathered her papers and began to leave. He put one hand around her wrist, the other around her waist, and began to push her out of the building. Mary went straight to the local police station and filed charges against Baker, claiming he violated her rights as a citizen.

The court agreed with Mary, but accounts of the incident made national news. Most reports poked fun at Mary for her behavior; others claimed that she responded to Baker by waving a gun at him. The slander and exaggerations were designed to portray Mary in the worst possible light and would be a pattern in newspaper accounts for years to come. Mary had a temper, to be sure, but it is improbable that she told Baker to "go to hell" as the *Hartford Courant* reported.

As the public and her sister suffragists became increasingly hostile toward her, Mary responded by stepping up her dress reform game. She cut her hair in a style popular with men at that time. She ditched her remaining ruffles and ribbons in favor of a more tailored look. Instead of an overcoat that flared at the bottom like a skirt, she now wore a straight overcoat with straight-legged pants. She sat for a portrait, in which the painter A. P. Hubbell captured her new look, and had several photographs taken. Perhaps by dressing like a man, Mary was making the visual claim that she demanded all the respect and rights granted to men.

In 1878 Mary published her second book, *Unmasked, or the Science of Immorality: To Gentlemen.* Although the author was credited only as "A Woman Physician and Surgeon," Mary readily acknowledged that she was the author. The book was a shockingly frank discussion of human sexuality. She wrote in her introduction that since so many male doctors had written books for women, she supposed that "men generally may be benefited by women physicians writing 'private treatises' to men, embodying advice, facts, observations, discoveries, etc., that are all important for men to learn in a pure way as matters of science, instead of acquiring with the most degraded ideas of life, and only such parts as are demoralizing and filled with the grossest errors."

Mary wore multiple styles of reform dress in her life. By the 1870s, she wore clothing that was much closer to the male fashions of the day than the women's fashions.

With the book, Mary wanted to shine a light on the double standards that men and women were held to when it came to sex and to guide men back to the "right path" of morality. "Men will be better," she wrote, "when the true principles of life are fully *unmasked*."

The strange book included chapters on masturbation, menstruation, and female anatomy. She believed that masturbation and shaving one's beard caused low sperm count in men so they would have a harder time having children. She disapproved of kissing because it spread diseases and aroused "animal passions" in men. She even devoted a chapter to hermaphrodites—people who are born with both male and female sexual organs (today they are described as intersex). Although she was sympathetic to their situation, she used the offensive (but common at the time) phrase "freak of nature" to describe them. She believed that hermaphrodism was the result of sexual or emotional abuse of a mother during her pregnancy.

Mary included some sex-positive views about women's sexuality. She wrote that a woman's menstrual cycle was designed to intensify her sexual excitement. She insisted that men who forced sex on their wives were guilty of rape. She concluded with a chapter on "The Language of Nerves," in which she said it would be in a couple's best interest for the woman to initiate sex when she was in the mood. She made the argument that a woman should have *supreme control of her person*."

That fall, Mary received the $900 she was owed for showing up to work every day at the Treasury Department. The money allowed her to buy the family property and home in Oswego Town, which her family had been renting out. It was important to her that she would be able to own and return to her childhood home.

CHAPTER 8

DIFFICULT TIMES

MARY WAS STILL LIVING IN WASHINGTON, DC, when she received the heartbreaking news that, on April 9, 1880, her father, Alvah, had died on his eighty-second birthday. He had always encouraged and supported Mary and her unconventional ways. His funeral was held two days later, and although there is no record that Mary was able to attend, a large number of friends and neighbors were there to say goodbye.

Mary's brother, Alvah Jr., read a tribute to their father, saying, "He was determined to maintain his individuality. . . . He never allowed another to do his thinking. But being a devoted reader, he read for himself, and no popularity or unpopularity could deter him from expressing that thought regardless of consequences." Alvah Jr. could have been describing his older sister Mary, so well did she absorb their father's lessons and apply them to her own life.

That summer, still grieving for her father and discouraged by the lack of progress in women's rights, Mary took a much-needed vacation in the Adirondack Mountains in upstate New York. On the train back to DC in September, a group of male passengers gave her a hard time about her clothing. They filled the train car with tobacco smoke just to irritate her. But when they learned that she was none other than the famous Dr. Mary Walker, they asked her to share her ideas.

Always delighted to have an audience, she gave an off-the-cuff lecture about the health benefits of her reform dress and the medical reasons she opposed tobacco. She won her tormentors over with her charm and intelligence—quite a difference from the angry, confrontational woman often described in the press. When they arrived in DC, she offered to give them a tour of the city and even introduced them to the vice president. That evening she hosted a party, which the press deemed a great success.

Mary's relationship with her brother, Alvah Jr., had been strained in recent years. He was, by all accounts, a difficult man, often at odds with the rest of his family. Mary did not help matters that fall when she filed a disability pension claim for her brother's service in the army. Describing herself as Alvah Jr.'s "dearest friend," she claimed he was not of his right mind due to sunstroke he had suffered during the war. The pension office rejected the claim, saying that his work habits, appearance, and "mental eccentricities" had not changed much from before the war. In other words, he had always been a little strange. Mary may have been trying to help her brother, but her actions sent him into a rage. Alvah Jr. challenged in court Mary's right to some of the property she had inherited from their father. He was unsuccessful, but it further tested their relationship.

It must have been awkward when Mary returned to Oswego Town on Election Day that fall, since Alvah Jr. lived next door to the family home she had purchased from their parents. But attempting to vote in her hometown had become a proud tradition for Mary. As usual, she was turned away from the polls because she was not a male citizen. "I am a fe-male citizen and therefore a male citizen," she told them. As she was leaving the polling place, a young man told her that she should get all the women in town to dress as men and attempt to vote. "I don't wear men's clothes," she declared. "I wear my own clothes."

When she bought the family home, part of the deal was that Mary would help support her mother and allow her to live in the house. Mary and her mother had always been close, and they both welcomed the arrangement. But Vesta was old and needed more help than Mary could provide, since she was often in DC. So Vesta moved in with Alvah Jr., who saw his opening. He told reporters that "Mary was so eccentric and whimsical that the old lady found it impossible to reside with her, and went to live with her daughter . . . and demanded that Dr. Mary should support her there." The newspaper reported that Mary refused to do so because she was only bound to support Vesta in her own home. Alvah Jr. also claimed that "on several occasions she has turned his horses into the road at night, and that he regards her as insane." The press was all too eager to paint Mary in a bad light.

Despite the negative press, Mary was determined to do her part to advance women's rights. Although she could not vote, in 1881 Mary declared herself a Democratic candidate for the US Senate for the state of New York. She had long supported the Republican Party as supporters of abolition, but she became disillusioned with their lack of progress on bringing the country back together after the Civil War. The years following the war had been economically difficult, with the Panic of 1873 resulting in plummeting wages for the working class.

Democrats responded by promising sound economic and fiscal policy. These ideas resonated with Mary, who had always been keenly invested in bettering the lives of working-class people. She wrote to the state legislature with a declaration of her candidacy, presenting a long list of her qualifications, including "her ability of a ready speaker on subjects of legislative import; her ownership of a brain that is never made abnormal by the use of anodynes [painkillers] or stimulants; her ignoring attire that destroys health, ruins morals, and deranges finance."

Unsurprisingly, Mary did not get the support she wanted. But she was the first woman in the United States to run for a seat in the Senate. Newspapers across the country carried the story.

Charles Guiteau was a staunch supporter of the Republican Party and campaigned in support of President Garfield. Believing he was instrumental to Garfield's election, he expected a job as a reward. When Garfield's staff refused, Guiteau began to think that the president was not fit for office.

Mary was in the public eye once again in 1882. On July 2, 1881, a man named Charles Guiteau shot President James Garfield. Guiteau, who had once been an ardent supporter of Garfield, became convinced that the president needed to be removed from office. Guiteau was arrested and jailed, and Garfield died of his injuries several months later. A friend of Mary's, Dr. Susan Edson, was one of his physicians.

In the trial that followed, Guiteau was convicted of murder

and sentenced to death. Mary, who had always been a staunch opponent of the death penalty, joined forces with his attorney, who argued that he should not be executed because he was mentally ill. Guiteau believed that it was God's will that he kill the president and wrote "I was God's man to do it."

This was not the first time, nor the last, that Mary used her medical expertise to weigh in on criminal cases. "I think it would be a burning disgrace to the country," she said, "if that man should be hanged. . . . He has shown himself to be insane throughout the trial. His hanging would disgrace me and all other citizens."

Mary worked hard to stop the execution, even going to the White House to try and convince President Chester Arthur, who took office after Garfield's death, to reconsider. But she was unsuccessful. Guiteau was executed on June 30.

On May 1, 1882, Mary landed a job as a mail-room clerk in the pension office of the Interior Department. She welcomed the additional money to supplement her meager pension income, and since her high profile ensured that her hiring would be reported in the press, she was pleased that the position raised public awareness of women holding government jobs. Best of all, she could wear her suitcoat and trousers.

Although she received a promotion in September of that year and her monthly evaluations were good, she did not get along with her supervisor, D. L. Gitt. He sought to fire her, saying she was "violent, high tempered and abusive . . . aggressive and insolent." He charged that she spent much of her time reading newspapers and writing personal letters and that she ate and slept at her desk during office hours. He claimed that Mary was lazy and had talked disrespectfully of the late president Garfield. Mary was anything but lazy, but she did admit saying that "President Arthur was a grand exchange for Garfield, as much as an assassination was to be deplored."

Mary, true to her nature, did not go quietly. She countered that Gitt and others in the office were lying about her performance because she had exposed hundreds of serious errors in handling the mail and insisted that the work be done correctly. What's more, Mary said, Gitt wanted to get rid of her because she knew he was having an affair with another female clerk in the office. She appealed to various government officials and even wrote a letter to President Arthur.

In the end, Gitt won. Mary was fired from her job in the summer of 1883, although she fought to reverse the dismissal for the next sixteen months.

In November 1886, the year Mary turned fifty-four, a young feminist, aspiring writer, and artist named Charlotte Perkins Gilman paid her a visit. Gilman was interested in learning more about women's health and women's rights. Two years earlier, at the age of twenty-four, Gilman had married the artist Charles Stetson. Their only child, Katharine Beecher Stetson, was born the following year. Gilman suffered severe postpartum (following childbirth) depression. Her doctor advised keeping the baby with her at all times, getting extensive bed rest, and never touching a pen, paintbrush, or pencil for the rest of her life. This "treatment" proved to be worse than the depression. Her experience inspired her now-famous 1890 short story

"The Yellow Wallpaper," which depicts a woman's descent into madness after being subjected to this "rest cure."

During her visit, Gilman and Mary discussed politics, marriage, and fashion. Gilman's marriage was rocky (Gilman and Stetson would separate in 1888 and divorce in 1894), and they most likely talked about the unequal legal procedures for men and women seeking to end their marriages. They agreed on many things, but Mary's laser focus on trousers for women was too much for Gilman, who wrote in her diary, "Like her,

Charlotte Perkins Gilman was a firm believer that women should not be confined to the domestic roles they held in the 1800s. Later in her life, she would give lectures on social reform and economic independence for women.

but am not converted. She has no feeling for beauty in costume; thinks it beneath intelligent beings." Later, she would write, "She was a competent physician, I understand, and a brave, good woman, but no human intellect can maintain its balance on so small a topic as the redistribution of trousers." In October of that year, Gilman had released "Why Women Do Not Reform Their Dress" in the suffrage publication *Woman's Journal*. She stressed, "To offend and grieve instead of pleasing, to meet opposition and contempt instead of praise and flattery, to change pride for shame,—this is suffering which no woman will accept unless it is proved her duty. And this is why women do not reform their dress."

★ ★ ★

Mary received the news that her mother had died on April 25, 1887. Vesta was eighty-five years old and had been in ill health for several years. Alvah Jr. had prepared to give a tribute at her funeral, but "for reasons that reflect no credit upon them," he wrote, the ministers did not allow him to speak. It's not clear why this happened, but Alvah Jr. was known to be an outspoken agnostic—he did not believe in any god. At any rate, he was justifiably irked when the local Oswego newspaper's obituary identified Vesta as the "mother of Dr. Mary Walker," omitting the names of her other children.

By 1887 it had been years since Mary had had a regular source of income. To earn some money, Mary signed on with a Chicago-based agency that produced stage lectures and exhibitions in "dime museums" across the country. Dime museums

The performers at dime museums varied from people with dwarfism (short stature) and people with gigantism (tall stature) to people with unusual skills and lecturers.

were popular (and cheap) centers for entertainment and education for the working class. For one dime, people could view stuffed two-headed calves, Peruvian mummies, shrunken heads, and a variety of other curiosities. They could also attend stage performances and lectures given by celebrities. The famous escape artist Harry Houdini got his start in dime museums; the sharpshooting frontierswoman Calamity Jane was a popular performer. Mary agreed to become a lecturer. She earned $150 a month (the equivalent of $4,388 today) speaking on topics like "Curiosities of the Brain," "Human Electricity," "Causes of Unusual People," "Beauties, Uses and Injuries of Tobacco," "Science of Dress," "Woman's Franchise," and "The Great Labor Question."

Some newspapers were critical of Mary's appearances at such "low-brow" venues. An article in the *Toledo Blade* was titled

Dr. Mary Walker
From the Platform of Princes
To the Stage of Freaks.

It went on to say, "There was a time when this remarkable woman stood upon the same platform of Presidents and the world's greatest women. There is something grotesque in her appearance on the stage built for freaks." Mary's response revealed her sense that all people are equal and deserving of respect. She told the *New York Times,*

> *I am of the opinion that the crying need of the masses is a better and more thorough scientific education than they at present receive. Now, you may think it strange that the first woman in the country*

to assert her right to vote, the first woman in the
country to vote in a political caucus, the first female
surgeon to serve in an army . . . should lecture in
a dime museum, but I tell you the time is not far
distant when the greatest scientists in the country
will adopt the stage of a dime museum as the best
place from which to disseminate knowledge. I want
to instruct a class of people who cannot afford to
patronize high-priced lectures.

In a national poll taken the year before, Mary was named the third-greatest social reformer in America—behind Susan B. Anthony and Frances Willard (a temperance reformer and suffragist), who tied for first. But in the coming years, Mary would be increasingly excluded from the mainstream suffrage movement and written out of its history. It was her attire and outspokenness the movement objected to, not her ideas.

In the early fall of 1887, the NWSA presented a document to President Grover Cleveland titled "Protest against the Unjust Interpretation of the Constitution." The document essentially used the same argument Mary had been promoting in her *Crowning Constitutional*

Frances Willard was elected president of the Woman's Christian Temperance Union in 1879 and served until her death in 1898. She was instrumental in the passage of the Eighteenth Amendment, which prohibited the sale of alcohol, and was a strong supporter of the Nineteenth Amendment, which granted women the right to vote.

Argument for the previous fifteen years. Signed by the current leadership of the organization, the document made no mention of Mary.

A few months later, her old friend Belva Lockwood publicly distanced herself from Mary, saying that she had no sympathy for her style of dress or her ideas on suffrage. It must have been terribly painful for Mary.

At the end of October 1888, in preparation for the upcoming presidential election, Mary published an appeal to "the great sisterhood all over to the land. . . . Sisters, step into your own ballot sphere, and the day is near when all men will arise and call you blessed."

That next spring, Mary walked, uninvited, onto the floor of the House of Representatives and approached the Speaker's desk. The representatives watched in shock as she told them that it would not be long before the Speaker of the House would be a woman and that she would recognize not the "gentleman from Indiana" but the "*lady* from Indiana." She continued to speak until the doorkeeper arrived to escort her from the hall. Mary was the first woman to *speak* from the desk of the Speaker of the House. Despite Mary's prediction, Americans would have to wait until 2007 to see Nancy Pelosi become the first female Speaker of the House of Representatives.

In the spring of 1889, Mary fell and broke her leg. When she fell again, Mary was confined to her bed for months. In an interview with a reporter, Mary let her guard down to reveal just how much her relentless activism had cost her. "The world has thought me hardened and brazen," she admitted. "I have never seen the day when it was not a trial to me to appear in public in a reform dress. Every jeer has cut me to the quick. Many times have I gone to my room and wept after being publicly derided. No one knows, or will ever know, what it has cost me to live up to my principles, to be consistent with my convictions and declarations; but I have done it and am not sorry for it."

In an April 1890 interview, she talked with reporter Robert Graves from her bed in a cramped attic room in Washington, DC. He wrote that she wore a loose-fitting blouse with a tie and looked pale and wan, her eyes tired. "I am alone, helpless, penniless, and no one will help me. It is a shame and an outrage the way this government has treated me!" she told the reporter, who concluded by saying that "her life has been one of sacrifice and of devotion to her idea of principle. . . . When well Dr. Walker supports herself very nicely by practicing medicine and lecturing. But it is not likely she will ever be able to work again."

The timing of these interviews was likely not coincidental. The government had enacted the Dependent Pension Act in June 1890, allowing veterans who could not perform manual labor to receive pensions. Because of her injury, Mary had applied for an increase in her pension, but in September Congress denied her application. Mary believed this decision was due to her reform dress and outspokenness. She hoped the interviews would bolster her case.

Alvah Jr.'s death at the age of fifty-six on May 17 may have contributed to her urgency to receive her rightful compensation from the government before she died. To Mary, being awarded a pension was less about the money—although she desperately needed it—and more about the recognition and acknowledgment she felt she deserved.

That next month, some of Mary's friends from New York nominated her as an independent candidate for Congress. She accepted the nomination, but New York's election laws prevented her name from appearing on the ballot. If she had been younger and healthier, she might have pursued her campaign with more vigor, but her slowly healing leg kept Mary to her bed. She spent much of the winter of 1890–1891 in Oswego Town, rarely leaving her house.

Mary eventually recovered, and in the coming years her interest in Democratic Party politics increased. In June 1892, she was selected to represent Oswego at the Democratic National Convention in Chicago. Grover Cleveland, representing the Republican Party, was running for president against the Democratic governor of New York, David Hill. Mary had no voting rights at the convention, but she was happy to show her support for Hill, standing on a chair and waving her handkerchief in support of her candidate. Susan B. Anthony attended the convention as well, but the women carefully avoided each other.

Mary turned sixty in November 1892, and in February 1893 she treated herself to a few weeks in New York City and a performance at the Imperial Music Hall. A reporter from the *New York Times* joined her in her private box, where she expressed her support for actresses, who were usually held in low regard by society, often thought to be prostitutes. "Now these poor girls who have to work so hard for a living have relatives," she told the reporter. "There is that young lady who sings naughty songs. She does it for a livelihood. She's got a sweet face, and she looks like a dear little woman. Bah! for the opinions of society."

By this time, Mary was wearing clothes much closer to men's fashion of the time than women's. She kept her hair short and wore long overcoats over straight leg trousers.

Mary gave a series of lectures in New York City about crinolines, the stiff petticoats used to make women's skirts bell out. The attire had recently come back into fashion. She noted that crinolines were prone to swaying up as women climbed onto streetcars or getting blown up in the wind, exposing women's legs. She poked fun at their size, saying, "Why, rapid transit will be impossible; ten women will fill up a car, men will get tripped up, and all sorts of trouble will follow if hoopskirts become the fashion."

She published an essay around this time, "Why Women Should Wear Trousers," insisting that "no woman is out of her doll-babyhood who is in petticoat trammels [shackles] instead of trousers."

In 1894 Mary began a campaign against the death penalty, giving lectures on the subject in Boston, Massachusetts. She had always opposed the death penalty, but her interest in the issue had intensified after the Guiteau case. She decried public hangings, which many people attended as a form of entertainment. Capital punishment will never prevent crime, she declared, an argument that most modern legal scholars agree with. She was also concerned about the execution of innocent people. Executions, she believed, were just state-sanctioned murders. She wanted people convicted of murder to serve life sentences in prison.

As a spiritualist, Mary also thought that "the spirit of an executed man will do all the harm it can for sake of glorying over its revenge." She advocated for rehabilitation rather than revenge for those who were imprisoned: "A person should be confined only for the sake of safety of his fellows. He should work for his own support and that of his family. He should be surrounded by flowers and pictures, and above all good books, so that when he gets his freedom, either by pardon or death, he will not leave with feelings of hostility to humanity." Mary, who once cooled herself with a fan bearing an image of the American flag in the wretched Castle Thunder, well understood how small comforts could offer a balm to the prisoner's soul.

Mary had begun spending more of her time in Oswego, and in 1895 she announced an ambitious new plan to advance women's causes. She would create a colony for women, a community where women could achieve economic independence. She hoped to purchase an additional 100 acres (40 ha) next to the 35 acres (14 ha) she already owned and build a farmhouse large enough for seventy-five women, with bathrooms, steam heat, and "every convenience to be found in a well-regulated and modern house."

Women would be expected to commit to living in the community for three years, working on the farm, and receiving a share of the profits. Mary proposed that these women would receive a university-level education and learn how to govern themselves. She said that all members of the community would be expected to wear reform dress and that when they rode horses, they "will astride, as do the men." Women's long skirts prevented them from riding astride horses; instead, they rode on a special sidesaddle. The colony would become, Mary predicted, "a perfect garden of Eden, but without the Adam."

REMINISCENCES

Mary kept a collection of complimentary things said and written about her, which she wrote down in her own handwriting. She didn't attribute any of the quotes to speakers or writers, or date them, but—assuming she didn't make them up in a fit of self-promotion—they must have been a morale booster when so many others were attacking or belittling her. Here are a few:

- "Dr. Mary E. Walker is not a giant, nor as old as Methuselah, nor as strong as Sampson, and yet—everybody rushes to see what she has to say about the prominent topics of the age."
- "No American woman has ever been honored and dinnered by scientific titled, and literary people as she has been, said a person when speaking of Dr. Mary E. Walker."
- "Dr. Mary E. Walker says, the public do not like to hear of any prominent person being ill like other mortals, unless they are likely to make a funeral entertainment for them."
- "Dr. Mary E. Walker is often taken for a clergyman, and especially of the Catholic church, owing to her smooth face."
- "Not only seven cities claimed Dr. Mary E. Walker as a native (as that number did of Homer), but more than twice seven states claimed her during the War."
- "Dr. Mary E. Walker will sometime be missed, as no American will be for a hundred years to come."

Her plan was widely publicized, although much of the coverage was mocking, but her feminist utopia was never realized. She did not have enough money to create the colony, but perhaps more devastating was the fact that there was little interest in joining or funding what must have seemed like an aging woman's pipe dream.

★ ★ ★

In February 1898, Mary suffered one final smackdown from the leaders of the National Women's Suffrage Association. She had not been to one of their conventions for years, but she decided to attend that year, despite not being invited, because she was already in DC and the event marked the fiftieth anniversary of the Seneca Falls Convention. When Susan B. Anthony presented the pioneers of the movement to the large audience, Mary was not among them. Later that day, Mary raised her hand to speak, but the meeting's chairwoman, Carrie Chapman Catt, cut her off with the rapping of her gavel. When she returned the next day, she found the doors locked. Mary believed that the organizers found her "such a forcible speaker, she will make these Delegates believe we have been on the wrong track all these years, and it is a question [between disgracing] *one* woman, or all us [being made] out simpletons" for pushing for a constitutional amendment.

A few days later, Mary spoke to some of the conference participants during a break in the proceedings, declaring, "Sue Anthony doesn't want suffrage for the women at all, for when they get it her occupation . . . will be gone." When her audience expressed shock at Mary's dubious claim, she replied, "You need not look so astonished for I know all about Sue Anthony . . . the love of power is the keynote of her character."

Carrie Chapman Catt (*center*) is pictured here with Helen Hamilton Gardener (*left*) and Maud Wood Park (*right*) on the balcony of the Suffrage House in Washington, DC. Though Catt joined the suffrage movement in the 1880s, she quickly became a popular lecturer for women's rights.

Mary explained that if Anthony and other suffragists had worked with her to try to get legislation passed acknowledging women's right to vote as citizens of the United States, women would have gained the right to vote fifteen years before. A reporter for the *St. Louis Globe-Democrat* wrote, "With her diminutive form drawn up to its full height, her eyes flashing and her face lit up with enthusiasm, [Mary] made the best argument for women's suffrage that I have heard." The reporter went on to write that as she listened to Mary, she forgot all about women's supposed inferiority or appropriate dress for women, "forgot everything but Dr. Walker's eloquence, and at the conclusion of her speech I went and shook hands with her and patted her on the back."

When the convention was over, the NWSA refunded Mary's annual dues. She was no longer welcome in the organization. Adding insult to injury, Mary was snubbed by the Daughters of the American Revolution (DAR) later that month. Mary could trace her family's history of service in the Revolutionary War, a requirement for any woman wishing to join the organization. She had filled out the paperwork for admittance and paid the required fee several months earlier, but at the group's annual convention that month, the board of management "decided that this society, being one composed of women, could not consider the candidate as eligible or acceptable, she having repudiated the recognized apparel of women." The DAR returned her papers and application fee.

CHAPTER 9

REFORMER TO THE END

MARY MAY HAVE BEEN BADLY TREATED by the leadership of the NWSA, but she also must have taken pride in the fact that a major newspaper in the nation's capital hailed her as "a remarkable woman" who still had a great deal of work to do.

She had very specific work in mind, as DC was soon to learn.

In 1893 Queen Kamakaeha Lili'uokalani, the last monarch of Hawai'i, was overthrown by a US-backed party of sugar- and pineapple-growing business owners. They had built profitable plantations on the islands, and set up a provisional government that would protect their financial interests. The president of the new government was Sanford Dole, of the Dole pineapple company. Dole put into place a constitution that granted voting rights based on wealth. After being held prisoner in her palace for eight months, the queen was released and kept on as a powerless, ceremonial head of the new government. They forced Native Hawai'ians off their land and prohibited them from teaching their language and practicing their cultural traditions, such as the hula dance. In 1897 the Dole government called on the United States to annex Hawai'i as a territory, arguing that the islands should serve as a fueling station and naval base for US military operations in the Pacific.

Mary strongly objected to annexation. She wrote a letter to the editor of the *Washington Post* explaining her position. She noted that when the United States had annexed Louisiana, Florida, and Alaska, "no rulers were dethroned in our acquisition of territory adjacent to our own, and peaceable negotiations were had with Spain and Russia in such purchases." But the forcible annexation of Hawai'i, she argued, meant "departing from republican justice to a small sister nation with which we were at peace," calling the action "highway robbery."

She also invited members of the Senate Committee on Territories to attend a lecture on why the United States should not annex Hawai'i. Not a single member attended, although several reporters did. One of them wrote that their absence was "proof of the degeneration of the United

Queen Kamakaeha Lili'uokalani was born in Hawai'i in 1838 and took the throne after her brother's death in 1891. She surrendered to the armed militia set up by the plantation owners to avoid bloodshed. She was a fierce advocate for a peaceful return to Hawai'ian sovereignty until her death in 1917.

States Senate . . . that not a single senator availed himself of this opportunity to acquire much useful information."

When Queen Lili'uokalani was in Washington, DC, to plead her case in January 1898, Mary requested a meeting with her. They met in the queen's rooms at a local hotel. Mary expressed sympathy for Hawai'i's political situation. Little else is known about what the two discussed. When their meeting was over, Mary bowed and kissed the queen's hand to show respect for her royal status.

In early February 1898, President William McKinley hosted President Dole at the White House. Mary asked for an invitation to the reception, citing her war record. It was granted, but not without some speculation amongst the press that Mary would cause a scene. She didn't.

Instead, the press focused on her conversation with the Chinese minister of foreign affairs. Wu Tingfang, the minister, had asked Mary why she wore pants. Politely, she answered, "Why do you wear a gown, or dress?" (She was referring to the traditional *changshan*, a long robe worn by Chinese men.)

The minister explained, "Because it is the custom of my country."

Wu Tingfang served as the minister of foreign affairs for China from 1897 to 1902 and 1907 to 1909. While in the United States, he gave numerous lectures about Chinese culture and history.

Mary countered, "Well, I wear trousers because this is a free country, and people are not handicapped by custom."

Mary lobbied members of Congress to vote no on the annexation of Hawai'i, insisting that Queen Lili'uokalani was "cruelly cheated out of her dominion [country]." That was a crime, she stated, committed in the name of the people of the United States: "Now we are asked to receive stolen property. Oh, it is a shame, a burning shame!"

Mary also published a pamphlet titled *Isonomy* (a term that means equality before the law), in which she further condemned annexation. She wrote,

> *What kind of example are lawmakers setting? If women were in their place they would not set such examples for their children, but would atone for the wrongs already suffered from a so-called Christian nation. . . . Never, in all time, and countries, have there been so many and various wrongs to civilized women, by the gentlemen, as since a great government has sanctioned and abetted the high-handed robbery of a Queen!*

The *Boston Globe* ran a lengthy article about Mary that spring, noting that she was "the only woman in the United States who wears trousers and doesn't wish she were a man." Mary told the reporter that some young women flirted with her with "brazen effrontery." It's not known whether Mary's clothing led them to believe she was a man, as was implied in the article, or whether they believed her clothing to be a signal that she was a lesbian. The latter possibility was surely too scandalous to be mentioned in a mainstream periodical. Mary also revealed that she had provided medical treatment to Chinese minister Wu's wife while they were in Washington, DC, and noted that Mrs. Wu wore "broadcloth pants and a tunic. She was dressed just about as I am." She explained, "I don't pretend to be a dude, and I don't care very much about following the latest styles."

When the US Senate met to vote on the annexation of Hawai'i in July, Mary was watching in the gallery, along with Queen Lili'uokalani and diplomatic representatives from around the world. The Senate adopted the annexation resolution by a vote of 42 to 21. Mary protested the vote with a wave of her white handkerchief, which earned her an ejection from the Senate gallery.

In the 1890s, US author Henry James popularized the phrase "New Woman" to describe the growing number of feminist, educated, independent, and professional women in the United States and Europe. By then, women's trousers had become known as "Mary Walkers," and bloomers were enjoying something of a resurgence with the new bicycling craze, since women couldn't ride bicycles wearing long, heavy dresses. Due to her advanced age, Mary was sometimes called the old New Woman, and she was the perfect target for those who were alarmed by these developments.

In 1899 a murder case making headlines in New York captured Mary's attention. Roland Molineux's family had made a fortune in the chemical dye business, and by the time he was thirty, he had developed a reputation as a vain playboy. In 1898 Molineux fell in love with a young woman named Blanche

Cheeseborough, who happened to have another suitor, Henry Barnet. In November of that year, Barnet received a package in the mail containing an over-the-counter stomach remedy made by a well-known drug company. Barnet, thinking he had received a free sample, took the medicine—and promptly fell ill and died. Fewer than two weeks later, Molineux and Cheeseborough were married.

Raised by wealthy parents, Roland Molineux (*above*) was quite snobbish and looked down on lower-class people. He also had a temper, which lead to his demanding the Knickerbocker Athletic Club expel Harry Cornish.

In December the athletic director of the exclusive Knickerbocker Athletic Club, Harry Cornish, beat Molineux in a weight lifting competition. Humiliated, Molineux demanded that the club management fire Cornish, which it declined to do. Later that month, Cornish received a bottle containing a popular liquid headache medicine. He gave it to his aunt, Katharine Adams, who took the medication and died after a bout of painful convulsions.

An investigation showed that the headache medicine was laced with cyanide. Based on handwriting analysis, the authorities matched Molineux's signature with that of the person who had signed the prescription for the poison-laced medicine. Molineux was found guilty and sentenced to death.

Although the indirect evidence seemed to point to Molineux's guilt, Mary believed it was insufficient to convict the man of murder. In mid-February 1899, she spoke before a committee of the New York State Assembly regarding Assemblyman John Maher's bill to abolish the death penalty in New York. She used the Molineux case to argue that capital punishment in this or any other case was not justified. "Murderers," she declared, "at the time of the commission of the crime, are in a trench of insanity, or in a never properly balanced condition, and should be the pitiable wards of state protection [imprisoned], instead of candidates for a chair of state electrocution." The bill never made it out of committee, and the death penalty remained law in New York.

Molineux spent twenty months on death row. After two appeals, he was eventually acquitted of the murder and released. Mary and other opponents of the death penalty were elated.

On May 13, 1900, at the age of seventy-five, Mary's sister Aurora collapsed on her kitchen floor and died. Of all her sisters, Mary was closest to Aurora, who had been married to a wealthy farmer. When she was living in Oswego Town, Mary had seen Aurora every day, and when she was out of town, her sister helped take care of her few farm animals and house. When she learned of her sister's death, Mary rushed home, arriving in the middle of the funeral service. She quietly placed a bouquet of flowers on her sister's coffin. Mary spent the rest of the summer in Oswego, grieving for her sister.

Mary threw herself back into presidential election campaigning that fall. She disliked President McKinley's abuse of power, especially his involvement in the annexation of Hawaiʻi and for his responsibility for the thousands of civilians who died of violence, famine, and disease in the Philippines during the Spanish-American War (1898). She supported the Democratic candidate, William Jennings Bryan, and traveled around New York campaigning for him. To Mary's dismay, McKinley was reelected in November.

Mary returned to Oswego in the summer of 1901. Weeks later, McKinley was shot and killed by Leon Czolgosz, the son of Polish immigrants and an anarchist who believed that government is both harmful and unnecessary. After a jury found Czolgosz guilty of murder, Mary made a remark at a New York train station that got her into big trouble. She said that the "State of New York if it electrocutes the assassin of McKinley is just as great a murderer as he is. President McKinley was a murderer, because he killed the poor Filipinos." After hearing her comment, a group of laborers surrounded Mary and threatened her, saying she should be lynched (put to death by a mob) or put into an insane asylum. The story ran in newspapers across the country.

Though he was highly criticized for his policies regarding the Spanish-American War, McKinley is credited with ushering the United States toward being more active in world affairs.

Mary defended herself, declaring that she did not believe in murder of any kind, either by "assassination, hanging or electrocuting, in the United States, the Philippine Islands, or anywhere else." Nevertheless, the public was outraged, and she was called out as a traitor. New York State suffragists banned her from their convention in October, and a US marshal was sent to New York to investigate her loyalty to the nation. The army threatened to rescind her pension. Nevertheless, Mary continued her efforts to prevent Czolgosz's execution. She was unsuccessful, and he was put to death on October 29, 1901. The intense national criticism of Mary died down soon after.

At the dawn of the twentieth century, Mary continued her activism in state and national politics, anti–death penalty advocacy, and women's rights. She spoke out against the new president, Theodore Roosevelt, who favored US expansion and control over other nations even more than McKinley.

In those early years of the twentieth century, the suffrage movement lost its two great leaders: Elizabeth Cady Stanton died in 1902, at the age of eighty-six, and Susan B. Anthony, also eighty-six, died four years later. One of Mary's good friends and a fellow dress reformer, Mary Tillotson, also died. In 1904 Mary learned that her sister Vesta had died. Mary was now among the last survivors of her generation of women's rights advocates. With most of the old guard gone, she continued to criticize the new generation of women suffragists who fought for a constitutional amendment. She claimed their amendment bills were "silly rubbish."

CROSSING THE GENDER LINE

Although Mary probably wouldn't have used the word *cross-dresser*, that is certainly what she was. And while she was scarcely the first cross-dresser in history (fifteenth-century Frenchwoman Joan of Arc cut her hair and donned a suit of armor to liberate the city of Orléans, France, from the English), she became the voice of cross-dressers. People whose choice of clothing did not reflect their biological gender increasingly sought her out.

In 1905 Mary offered to give Frank Williams a place to recover at her house in Oswego Town after Williams fell ill in Cincinnati. Born Frances Lamouche, they had been working as a hotel barber and had dressed in male clothes since childhood. Frank's biological gender was only discovered when they were hospitalized. While many people condemned Frank for "disgracing" their sex, Mary wrote to them, saying, "You need not be afraid to wear boy's clothing here. We dress to suit our inclinations, and the fact that you have discarded the horribly conventional clothing of women shows you to be a woman of more than ordinary intelligence, and consequently worthy of championship."

It does not seem to have occurred to Mary that Frank may have worn male attire not for comfort or health but because they identified as a man. Nor does it appear that Frank took Mary up on her offer to recover at her house in Oswego Town.

Mary was somewhat less supportive of Professor Randolph Milbourne of Ohio, perhaps because their stated preference for women's clothing, including corsets, ran counter to Mary's argument against fashionable women's attire. Milbourne had lived publicly as a man for decades but had wanted to be a woman since childhood. At home they lived and dressed as a woman, but it was not until 1905 that they gathered the courage to venture outside dressed in female clothing. Milbourne was arrested, so they wrote a letter to the attorney general. "For years I have worn ladies' garments about my home and I feel much better than when dressed as a man," they wrote. "While physically I am a man, yet spiritually and intellectually I am neither a man nor a woman, while I feel that in form and spirit I incline more to effiminancy and am gradually taking on more of the nature of womanhood."

In the letter, Milbourne used Mary as an example: "If Dr. Mary Walker can lawfully wear men's clothing upon the streets of American cities, why should not I be allowed to wear women's garments if I prefer to do so? Another thing: my form is better suited for female dress than for male attire, and I never feel comfortable in men's clothing, while I am at perfect ease when dressed as a woman. For ten years I have worn a woman's corset, and could scarcely live without it." Milbourne closed by noting that they were sixty-one years old, had fought for the Union army, and "no one will go further than I will to stand by the law of the land."

Milbourne decided to challenge their arrest in court, but when the attorney general declined to advise them, they contacted Mary. Mary told Milbourne that there might be an issue of "disguise," referring to a law prohibiting people from disguising their true nature, at stake here and could offer them no other advice.

Doctors of this era classified cross-dressing and other gender nonconforming behavior as a disease. They invented the term *sexual inversion* to describe someone who adopted the appearance and actions of the opposite gender. A former assistant surgeon in the Union army, Dr. Joseph Richardson Parke, speculated in his book on human sexuality that Mary suffered from "delusional masculinity."

In 1906 Mary was rushed to the hospital with a severe respiratory illness. She had suffered chronic bronchitis ever since she was imprisoned at Castle Thunder, and it got worse as she aged. In the hospital, she insisted on being her own doctor. "All I want is a room here in the hospital until I get well," she said.

The nurses liked Mary. "She is just as good a woman as any of us," one nurse noted. Still, the anti–New Woman crowd pointed to her ability to care for herself as a "masculine trait." Mary recovered and was soon back to work.

Mary had long wanted to build a tuberculosis sanatorium (a medical facility to treat the respiratory disease) on her property. In an attempt to raise money for such an institution, she had published a pamphlet, *Consumptive School Sanitarium* (tuberculosis was commonly called consumption at the time). Mary explained that her years as a successful physician qualified her to be its director and revealed that she herself had suffered from tuberculosis and had made a full recovery.

Although Robert Koch had discovered the bacteria responsible for tuberculosis in 1882, Mary and many other physicians at that time were slow to embrace the germ theory of disease. Most doctors thought the best treatment for tuberculosis was fresh air, moderate exercise, and a healthy diet, and in fact these treatments were useful. Her property in Oswego Town offered fresh air "away from city noises and smoke . . . where there is natural lime-water, vegetables right out of the ground, and from stalks, vines and bushes; fruit also fresh vines, trees and bushes; milk fresh from individual cows; eggs newly laid; clothes dried in sunshine, growing fruits, and flowers to watch and tend."

Mary stressed that every patient, rich or poor, would have "the comforts and attractions essential to treatment and education of consumptives." Mary didn't receive the funding she sought for her sanatorium, although she did offer her farm as a retreat for the occasional tuberculosis patient.

A few years later, an accomplished musician named Waldorf advertised for a "living right index finger" to replace the one she had lost in an accident. Waldorf stated that she was independently wealthy and was willing to pay almost anything for a finger that could be grafted onto her hand.

Mary jumped at the chance. Finally, a way to finance her sanatorium! She wrote to Waldorf:

> *I have just read that you desire to purchase a right index finger. Will you give me enough to erect a consumptive ward on my estate here? I have saved hopeless cases, and because I declare consumption is not contagious money is not forthcoming to erect a ward. I finish this letter not using my index finger.*
>
> *MARY E. WALKER, MD*
> *Surgeon in War of 1861–65*
>
> *P.S. If return ticket is sent I will come immediately so you can decide if my finger is desired by yourself.*   *DR. WALKER*

Newspapers across the country mocked Mary for thinking that a younger woman would want the finger of a seventy-nine-year-old woman, although none of them seemed to think that Waldorf's offer to buy a body part was strange. And Waldorf's surgeon declared that she needed a finger with dexterity and that Mary's finger was "altogether too old for our purposes."

When her sanatorium idea fell through, Mary had another idea for her farm. In a striking example of her humanitarianism, she offered to turn over her house and acreage to the county if it would use it to reform young prisoners. "My latest desire is again to try to better humanity," she told reporters. "Our penal institutions for old and young are, in my judgement, worthy of the days of the rack and the stake [torture devices]." Mary believed strongly in rehabilitation—restoring offenders to a law-abiding and useful place in society. At her proposed institution, each inmate "should be compelled to work a certain number of hours each day in the fields, and the remainder of his day should be spent in classrooms under the direction of the best teachers. Good clothes, neat linen, wholesome food, and plenty of it should be furnished."

Despite her own financial difficulties, Mary even offered to donate $10,000 (the equivalent of about $309,000 today) of her own money to help build the facility. The county considered her offer but in the end turned her down.

In 1912 Mary traveled to Chicago, where she spent four months lecturing. She angered many of the city's reformers when she criticized Jane Addams. She was the founder of Hull House, a facility that provided housing, education, and social activities to working-class immigrants. Addams, who would be awarded the

Nobel Peace Prize in 1931, was a feminist, peace activist, and social worker. She was one of the most highly regarded reformers in the country, yet Mary took issue with her support of Theodore Roosevelt. With characteristic bluntness, Mary said she "was at a loss to understand" how Addams could support Roosevelt, adding, "unless she was a crass seeker of popularity and publicity."

Addams shrugged off Mary's comments. "I don't mind," she said. "I'll just keep on with my work."

The suffrage organizations of Chicago, on the other hand, did not disregard Mary's insulting comment. Mary attended the Illinois state suffrage meeting, but the organizers ignored her.

In 1889 Jane Addams (*above*) established the Hull House with her friend Ellen Gates Starr after visiting a similar settlement house in London, England. She was an outspoken supporter of education and campaigned for better working conditions in factories. At the outbreak of World War I (1914–1918), Addams began promoting pacifism and protested the United States' involvement in the war.

In early February 1913, Mary, now eighty years old, was once again arrested for wearing men's clothing in public. As usual, she was released.

She continued to lecture on women's rights and labor rights for the next few years. In a discussion on marriage, she revived an old claim that President Chester Arthur had proposed to her not once, but twice, by letter. There is no way of knowing whether this is true, as Arthur's papers were destroyed at his request the day before he died. Some people thought the letters were not from President Arthur at all but were sent as a prank at Mary's expense, but Mary believed they were sincere. She turned him down, she said, primarily because he was a tobacco smoker, but she added, "I would not lose my identity in his. As his wife I would have been the first lady in the land for a few years and then would have been nobody as his widow. I will always be a somebody."

Although Mary generally disapproved of marches, believing them to be symbolic but not of much practical purpose, she agreed to head a section of marchers in a huge suffrage parade in New York City on October 24, 1915. The parade took place two weeks before a New York State referendum—which gives registered voters the chance to vote for or against a law—to give women the right to vote. She agreed to do so because the march was widely inclusive. According to a reporter for the *New York Evening World*, "Some whose names are to be found all through the Social Register [a listing of the city's wealthiest people] marched side by side with working mothers with babies in their arms. A large proportion of the marchers were young girls who would not be old enough to vote when they enfranchised." Thirty thousand women from twenty countries marched for four hours, from Washington Square to Central Park. It was the largest suffrage parade to date.

Although the referendum lost, the parade left a deep and lasting impression across the nation. Henry J. Allan, a newspaper editor from Kansas who watched the parade, wrote, "It was absolutely overwhelming. Forty thousand women do not spend days getting ready for a five-mile [8 km] march through crowded streets, and hours marching in a raw afternoon, for a transitory whim. It was the most dramatic exhibition I have ever seen in New York."

In 1917 Mary was back in Washington, DC. In April of that year, the United States declared war on Germany and joined the Allies in World War I. Mary, like many women, supported the peace movement. She sent a telegram to the German leader, Kaiser Wilhelm, calling on him to stop the war and offering him and other European leaders the use of her home on Bunker Hill Road in Oswego Town for a peace conference. Her only rules were that she would not permit alcohol or tobacco. Not surprisingly, she got no answer.

Around this time, Mary learned that the army's Medal of Honor board had revised the standards for earning the medal to include only "actual combat with an enemy . . . above and beyond the call of duty." Mary was among the 911 recipients whose Medal of Honor was rescinded. Mary petitioned the generals on the board to reconsider. Her petition was denied. Still, she refused to return her medal and wore it daily for the rest of her life.

Mary had intended to work for the Red Cross during the war, but she wouldn't get the chance. About a month after the United States entered the war, Mary was at the Capitol, likely trying to talk to an official about her Medal of Honor or her pension. She would later say that while she was on the steps outside the building, a gust of wind blew her over. In all likelihood, the eighty-five-year-old doctor simply fell. She broke her nose and three fingers. One knee and wrist were badly sprained. She returned to her home in Oswego Town to recuperate, but she never fully recovered.

Many of the last photos of Mary show her with a men's top hat. This photo was taken in 1911, in Washington, DC, eight years before her death.

Mary Walker died in her beloved Bunker Hill Road home on the morning of February 22, 1919. A neighbor who had been caring for Mary in her final months wrote that "her mind was clear and active" to the very end. She had lived a full life.

Years earlier, when she was sixty-four years old, Mary told a newspaper reporter, "If people want to know how old I am, I say I am nearly as old as Methuselah because we live in deeds and not in years." In the Christian bible, Methuselah is said to have lived 969 years.

Newspapers across the country, including the *New York Times*, published lengthy obituaries, praising her as a doctor who was a true patriot, war hero, and veteran, and a pioneering suffragist and women's rights activist. She was buried in a black formal suit in a flag-draped casket in the family plot next to her parents. Her Medal of Honor was given to the Oswego County Historical Society.

Her friend Dr. Bertha Van Hoosen said, "Dr. Mary's life should stand out to remind us that when people do not think as we do, do not dress as we do, and do not live as we do, that they are more than likely to be a half century ahead of their time, and that we should have for them not ridicule but reverence."

EPILOGUE

EIGHTEEN MONTHS AFTER MARY'S DEATH, on August 18, 1920, Congress ratified the Nineteenth Amendment. It recognized women as citizens of the United States and gave them the right to vote. It was not the solution that Mary had wished for, but she would have been proud to cast her vote.

Helen Hay Wilson had vague childhood memories of meeting her elderly great-aunt Mary Walker at her home on Bunker Hill Road. Wilson's grandmother, Mary's sister Luna, told Helen that if Mary had been a man, "they wouldn't have dared take her medal away."

In the 1960s, Wilson, along with a distant relative named Anne Miller, launched a campaign to have Mary's Medal of Honor reinstated. Their effort would take years, but they were as persistent as Mary had always been.

Their campaign came to a head in 1976 when the second wave of the women's movement was gaining steam. There was renewed interest in the Equal Rights Amendment (ERA), first introduced into Congress in 1923 by Alice Paul, the cofounder of the National Woman's Party.

ALICE PAUL AND THE EQUAL RIGHTS AMENDMENT

Alice Paul was among the women who helped secure passage of the Nineteenth Amendment. While many suffragists scaled back their activism after the enactment of the amendment, Paul believed that the true fight for equality had only begun. Paul, who had cofounded the National Woman's Party in 1912, began working on a new constitutional amendment that she originally named the Lucretia Mott Amendment, after the famous suffragist.

Renamed the Equal Rights Amendment and rewritten in 1943, the amendment called for absolute equality between men and women. The current version of the amendment reads, "Equality of rights under the law shall not be denied or abridged by the United States or by any state on account of sex."

Alice Paul had been campaigning for the passage of the Nineteenth Amendment for years before it was ratified in 1920. After the amendment became law, Paul turned her efforts toward gaining full equality for women.

The ERA was introduced in every session of Congress from 1923 until it finally passed in 1972 and was sent to the states for ratification. The ERA got twenty-two of the necessary thirty-eight state ratifications in the first year—and then the pace slowed.

Opponents of the ERA, led by conservative activist Phyllis Schlafly, argued that the amendment threatened traditional gender roles. They argued that the amendment would require women to fight in the military, take away protections such as alimony for divorced women, and require women to share bathrooms with men—none of which was true. They organized housewives to bring homemade jams and apple pies to lobby legislators, labeled with the slogans "Preserve us from a congressional jam: Vote against the ERA sham," and "I am for Mom and apple pie."

By June 20, 1982, the deadline for state ratifications, the ERA was three states short of the required thirty-eight. Activists continue to work for its ratification.

In a letter sent to a member of President Gerald R. Ford's staff in 1976, Anne Walker, a medical writer and a distant relative of Mary's, asked if she might have a meeting with President Ford and his wife, Betty, about Mary's medal. Walker wrote that she "must apply for some funds to help me live while finishing the 'campaign' [to restore Mary's medal]. . . . I am destitute without funds and have already expended a total of fourteen thousand dollars just to get the whole [process to] move this far." Concluding a letter that sounded very much like what Mary herself might have written, Walker lamented that bicentennial organizers had not funded her work, saying, "they have done nothing for science and/or medicine or women as a people!"

Wilson's and Walker's persistence paid off. In June 1977, the army secretary announced that the army had restored Mary

Walker's Medal of Honor. President Jimmy Carter formally reinstated Mary's medal, citing her "distinguished gallantry, self-sacrifice, patriotism, dedication and unflinching loyalty to her country, despite the apparent discrimination because of her sex." Mary is still the only woman to have been granted the Medal of Honor.

"I have a feeling of sadness," Anne Walker said, "that Dr. Mary died sixty years too early to witness the restoration of her medal. It was her misfortune to be one hundred years before her time."

This echoed what Mary Walker liked to say during her lifetime: "It is the times which are behind me."

AUTHOR'S NOTE

I STUMBLED UPON MARY EDWARDS WALKER when I was doing research on women scientists and doctors for another project. As I read about her, I was amazed to learn that she was one of the most famous women of her time, and yet hardly anyone knows about her today. I think it had a lot to do with her unwillingness to play nice and compromise her ideals. She annoyed and alienated a lot of people, even those who agreed with her on most issues. She was prickly and, I suspect, not easy to get along with. I may not always have agreed with her—I often found myself shaking my head or rolling my eyes in response to some of her ideas and stances—but I could never doubt her personal integrity, grit, and idealism, even as it came at great cost to her personal life, finances, and reputation.

I am indebted to the librarians at the Syracuse University Libraries, who granted me access to Mary Edwards Walker Papers in the Special Collections Research Center; at the Drexel University College of Medicine Legacy Center Archives and Special Collections on Women in Medicine and Homeopathy, for access to the Lida Poynter Collection; and at the National

Museum of Health and Medicine in Silver Spring, Maryland, for background information about Civil War medicine. To be able to hold in my hands and read documents and letters from the Civil War era was invaluable and humbling. I have retained the spelling and grammar of the letters of correspondence.

I found a great deal of original material online at Newspapers.com and in the excellent University of Illinois Library and the New York Public Library databases.

For those who wish to learn more about Mary Edwards Walker, I highly recommend two of my most valuable secondary sources, both highly readable biographies: *Dr. Mary Walker: An American Radical* by Sharon M. Harris and *Dr. Mary Walker's Civil War: One Woman's Journey to the Medal of Honor and the Fight for Women's Rights* by Theresa Kaminski.

And finally, many thanks to my wise editor Jesseca Fusco and my sharp-eyed copyeditor Stacy DeKeyser. The book is much better because of you.

SOURCE NOTES

7 "Miss Dr. Walker in Richmond," *Richmond Republic,* June 28, 1865; repr., *Cincinnati Daily Enquirer,* July 7, 1865.

7 Sharon M. Harris, *Dr. Mary Walker: An American Radical, 1832–1919* (New Brunswick, NJ: Rutgers University Press, 2009), 58.

8 Elizabeth D. Leonard, *Yankee Women: Gender Battles in the Civil War* (New York: W. W. Norton, 1994), 139.

8 "Miss Dr. Walker in Richmond," *Richmond Republic.*

8 "Miss Dr. Walker in Richmond."

8 "Miss Dr. Walker in Richmond."

8 "Miss Dr. Walker in Richmond."

8 Leonard, *Yankee Women,* 269.

12 Mercedes Graf, *A Woman of Honor: Dr. Mary Edwards Walker and the Civil War* (Gettysburg, PA: Thomas, 2001), 23.

17 "Report of the Woman's Rights Convention, Held at Seneca Falls, New York, July 19th and 20th, 1848. Proceedings and Declaration of Sentiments," printed by John Dick at the North Star Office, Rochester, NY, July 19–20, 1848, available online at the Library of Congress, https://www.loc.gov/resource/rbcmil .scrp4006702/?sp=10.

17 History.com editors, "Seneca Falls Convention," History.com, last modified March 9, 2022. https://www.history.com/topics/womens-rights/seneca-falls-convention.

17 Sally Gregory McMillen, *Seneca Falls and the Origins of the Women's Rights Movement* (New York: Oxford University Press, 2008), 93.

18 McMillen, 94.

18 "Bolting among the Ladies," *Oneida (Utica, NY) Whig*, August 1, 1848.

19 Allen D. Spiegel and Peter B. Suskind, "Mary Edwards Walker, MD: A Feminist Physician a Century Ahead of Her Time," *Journal of Community Health* 21, no. 3 (1993): 211.

19 Spiegel and Suskind, 211.

20 S. R. Charles, "The Only Self Made Man in America: A Talk with Dr. Mary Walker," *Minneapolis Sunday Tribune*, July 4, 1897.

21 Charles.

21 Charles.

22 "Commencement of Syracuse Medical College," *American Medical & Surgical Journal* 7, no. 4 (April 1855): 148.

23 "Commencement of Syracuse Medical College," 150–151.

23 Harris, *Dr. Mary Walker*, 12.

23 Harris, 12.

24 Lida Poynter, "Dr. Mary Walker, the Forgotten Woman" (unpublished manuscript, Drexel University College of Medicine, Archives and Special Collections on Women in Medicine and Philosophy), 34.

24 Poynter, 34.

25 Harris, *Dr. Mary Walker*, 16.

25 Harris, 16.

25 Charles, "The Only Self Made Man."

26 Gayle V. Fischer, *Pantaloons and Power: A Nineteenth-Century Dress Reform in the United States* (Kent, OH: Kent State University Press, 2001), 82.

27 "The Bloomer's Complaint," notated music (Philadelphia: A. Fiot, 1851), available online at the Library of Congress, https://www.loc.gov/item/sm1851.500460/.

27–28 Sharon M. Harris, "A New Style for Suffragists," *Humanities*, May/June 2006, 23.

28 Fischer, *Pantaloons and Power*, 103.

28 "Elizabeth Smith Miller," *New York History Net*, accessed May 20, 2022, http://www.nyhistory.com/gerritsmith/esm.htm.

28 Dexter C. Bloomer, *Life and Writings of Amelia Bloomer* (Boston: Arena, 1895), 72.

28 Mary Edwards Walker, *Hit* (New York: American News, 1871), 74.

31 Mary Edwards Walker, "Sickles and Key Tragedy," *Sibyl*, May 15, 1859, 553–554.

31 Walker, 553–554.

32 Mary Edwards Walker, "N. York State Foundling Hospital," *Sibyl*, August 1, 1859, 594.

32 Walker, 594.

33 Mary Edwards Walker, "Women Soldiers," *Sibyl*, September 1, 1859, 610–611.

33 Dale L. Walker, *Mary Edwards Walker: Above and Beyond* (New York: Forge, 2005), 70.

33 Theresa Kaminski, *Dr. Mary Walker's Civil War: One Woman's Journey to the Medal of Honor and the Fight for Women's Rights* (Guilford, CT: Lyons, 2020), 26, Google Books.

33–34 Kaminski, 26.

38 Louisa May Alcott, *Life, Letters, and Journals*, ed. Ednah D. Cheney (Boston: Little, Brown, 1898), 127, https://www.gutenberg.org/files/38049/38049-h/38049-h.htm#Page_136.

38 Harris, *Dr. Mary Walker*, 32.

40 Elizabeth D. Leonard, *Yankee Women: Gender Battles in the Civil War* (New York: W. W. Norton, 1994), 116.

40 Mary Edwards Walker, "Incidents Connected with the Army," Mary Edwards Walker Papers, Box 4, Special Collections Research Center, University Archives, Syracuse University Libraries.

40–41 Dale L. Walker, *Mary Edwards Walker: Above and Beyond*, 91.

41 Poynter, "Dr. Mary Walker, the Forgotten Woman," 53.

41 Poynter, 53.

41 Poynter, 53.

42 Walker, "Incidents Connected with the Army."

42 Elizabeth Conklin to Mary Edwards Walker, December 28, 1861, Box 1, 1861, Special Collections Research Center, University Archives, Syracuse University Libraries.

42 Conklin to Walker.

43 Edmund J. Danford to Mary Edwards Walker, February 1863, Box 1, 1863, Special Collections Research Center, University Archives, Syracuse University Libraries.

44 Thomas Kelly to Mary Edwards Walker, July 27, 1865, Special Collections Research Center, University Archives, Syracuse University Libraries.

44 Kaminski, *Dr. Mary Walker's Civil War*, 110.

45 Walker, "Incidents Connected with the Army."

46 Walker.

46 Walker.

46 Walker.

46 Graf, *A Woman of Honor*, 28.

46 Graf, 28.

46 Graf, 28.

47 Graf, 28.

47 Harris, *Dr. Mary Walker*, 34.

48 Mary Edwards Walker, draft of "On Washington," Special Collections Research Center, University Archives, Syracuse University Libraries.

49 Kaminski, *Dr. Mary Walker's Civil War*, 84.

49   Walker, "Incidents Connected with the Army."

50   Graf, *A Woman of Honor*, 30.

50   Walker, "Incidents Connected with the Army."

51   Walker.

51   Walker.

51   Kaminski, *Dr. Mary Walker's Civil War*, 92.

51   Kaminski, 92.

52   Walt Whitman, "The Wound-Dresser," Poetry Foundation, accessed May 20, 2022, https://www.poetryfoundation.org /poems/53027/the-wound--dresser.

52   Kaminski, *Dr. Mary Walker's Civil War*, 92.

53   Walker, "Incidents Connected with the Army."

53   Abraham Lincoln, "Preliminary Emancipation Proclamation," September 22, 1862, available online at the National Archives, https://www.archives.gov /exhibits/american_originals_iv/sections/preliminary _emancipation_proclamation.html.

54   Kaminski, *Dr. Mary Walker's Civil War*, 93.

54   Walker, "Incidents Connected with the Army."

54–55 Walker.

55   Harris, *Dr. Mary Walker*, 43.

55   Harris, 45.

56   Records of the War Department, Office of the Adjutant General, Record Group No. 94, National Archives and Records Administration, Washington, DC.

56   Records of the War Department.

56   Records of the War Department.

57   Kaminski, *Dr. Mary Walker's Civil War*, 123.

57   Elizabeth Leonard, *All the Daring of the Soldier: Women of the Civil War Armies* (New York: W. W. Norton, 1999), 217.

57   Kaminski, *Dr. Mary Walker's Civil War*, 124.

58   Roberts Bartholow, letter to the editor, *New York Medical Journal* 5 (1867): 169.

58 Mary Edwards Walker to President Johnson, September 30, 1865, Records of the War Department, Office of the Adjutant General, Record Group No. 94, National Archives and Records Administration, Washington, DC.

59 Walker, "Incidents Connected with the Army."

59 Walker.

60 Walker.

60 Walker.

62 Walker.

62 Walker.

62 Walker.

63 Walker.

63 Walker.

63 Walker; "Mrs. Dr. Mary Walker and a Suspicious Old Lady," *Cincinnati Daily Enquirer*, February 10, 1870.

63 Walker; "Mrs. Dr. Mary Walker."

63 Walker; "Mrs. Dr. Mary Walker."

63 Walker; "Mrs. Dr. Mary Walker."

64 Chris Enss, *The Pinks: The First Women Detectives, Operatives, and Spies with the Pinkerton National Detective Agency* (Guilford, CT: TwoDot, 2017), 133.

65 Harris, *Dr. Mary Walker*, 58.

66 Kaminski, *Dr. Mary Walker's Civil War*, 139.

66 Kaminski, 139.

66 Kaminski, 139.

66 Kaminski, 140.

68 "Dr. Mary Walker," *National Republican*, June 24, 1864.

68 Kaminski, *Dr. Mary Walker's Civil War*, 141.

68 Kaminski, 141.

69 *Richmond Examiner*, May 13, 1864.

69 Kaminski, *Dr. Mary Walker's Civil War*, 144.

69 Kaminski, 144.

69 Kaminski, 147.

70 Kayla M. Pittman, "From 'Invalid Corps' to Full Active Duty: America's Disabled Soldiers Return to War," National Museum of American History, accessed May 20, 2022, https://americanhistory.si.edu/blog/invalid-corps -full-active-duty-americas-disabled-soldiers-return-war.

70–71 Frank Wilder, "The Invalid Corps" (Boston: Henry S. Tolman, 1863), available online at the Library of Congress, https://www.loc.gov/item/ihas.200002281/.

73 Kaminski, *Dr. Mary Walker's Civil War*, 150.

73 Mary Edwards Walker to General Sherman, September 14, 1864, Dr. Mary Walker Papers, Oswego County Historical Society, Oswego, New York.

74 Frances Thomas Howard, *In and Out of the Lines: An Accurate Account of Incidents during the Occupation of Georgia by Federal Troops in 1864–65* (New York: Neale, 1905), 71.

74 Kaminski, *Dr. Mary Walker's Civil War*, 159.

75 Harris, *Dr. Mary Walker*, 65.

75 Harris, 65.

75 Cary Conklin letter, July 8, 1873, Special Collections Research Center, University Archives, Syracuse University Libraries.

75–76 Kaminski, *Dr. Mary Walker's Civil War*, 166.

76 Kaminski, 168.

76 "Last Public Address," Speeches and Writings, Abraham Lincoln Online, accessed May 20, 2022, http://www .abrahamlincolnonline.org/lincoln/speeches/last.htm.

76 "Last Public Address."

77 "Last Public Address."

77–78 Kaminski, *Dr. Mary Walker's Civil War*, 171.

78 Harris, *Dr. Mary Walker*, 71.

79 Albert Miller to Lyman Coats, July 19, 1865, Special Collections Research Center, University Archives, Syracuse University Libraries.

79 Miller to Coats.

79 Lydia Sayer Hasbrouck to Mary Edwards Walker, July 27, 1865, Special Collections Research Center, University Archives, Syracuse University Libraries.

79 Hasbrouck to Walker.

80 Erin Blakemore, "President Andrew Johnson Was Impeached for Firing a Cabinet Member," History.com, accessed May 20, 2022, https://www.history.com/news /andrew-johnson-impeachment-tenure-of-office-act.

81 "Mary E. Walker," Stories of Sacrifice, Congressional Medal of Honor Society, accessed May 20, 2022, https:// www.cmohs.org/recipients/mary-e-walker.

84 Charles McCool Snyder, *Dr. Mary Walker: The Little Lady in Pants* (New York: Vantage, 1962), 55.

84 G. Richmond to Mary Edwards Walker, August 13, 1866, Special Collections Research Center, University Archives, Syracuse University Libraries.

84 Richmond to Walker.

84 C. B. Brockway to Mary Edwards Walker, July 16, 1866, Special Collections Research Center, University Archives, Syracuse University Libraries.

85 An Act for the Relief of Mary E. Miller, State of New York, No. 623, March 15, 1866, Special Collections Research Center, University Archives, Syracuse University Libraries.

85 Harris, *Dr. Mary Walker*, 77.

85 Harris, 107.

86 Harris, 108.

86 US Const., amend. XIV, § 1.

87 US Const., amend. XIV, § 2.

88 Harris, *Dr. Mary Walker*, 82.

88 Harris, 82.

88 Harris, 82.

88 Harris, 82.

89 Kaminski, *Dr. Mary Walker's Civil War*, 199.

89 Kaminski, 200.

90   Harris, *Dr. Mary Walker*, 81.

90   Harris, 82.

90   Harris, 82.

90   "Police Trials: City Judge Russel, Mr. Charles S. Spencer, Dr. E.B. Dalton and Mrs. Dr. Mary E. Walker before Commissioners Acton, Bergen and Manierre," *New York Times*, June 14, 1866.

90   "Police Trials."

90   "Police Trials."

90–91   "The Dress Question," *Brooklyn Daily Eagle*, June 14, 1866.

91   "The Dress Question."

92   Harris, *Dr. Mary Walker*, 84.

93   Dennis Pitt and Jean-Michel Aubin, "Joseph Lister: Father of Modern Surgery," *Canadian Journal of Surgery* 55 no. 5 (October 2012): E8–E9.

94   Kaminski, *Dr. Mary Walker's Civil War*, 203.

95   "Dr. Mary Walker," *National Reformer*, December 9, 1866.

95   "Dr. Mary Walker."

95   Harris, *Dr. Mary Walker*, 91.

95   Harris, 91.

95–96   Harris, 88.

96   Snyder, *Dr. Mary Walker: The Little Lady in Pants*, 70.

96   Harris, *Dr. Mary Walker*, 89.

98   Snyder, *Dr. Mary Walker: The Little Lady in Pants*, 73.

98   Snyder, 73.

98   Snyder, 73.

98–99   Snyder, 74.

100   Eliza Cook, "The Old Arm-Chair," in *Melaia and Other Poems* (London: Charles Tilt, 1840), available online at poet.org, https://poets.org/poem/old-arm-chair.

100   Poynter, "Dr. Mary Walker, the Forgotten Woman," 66-67.

103   Harris, *Dr. Mary Walker*, 103.

104   "Pure Love and Sacred Marriage," *New York Tribune*, June 3, 1869.

105 "The Women's Rights Convention," *National Republican*, January 20, 1869.

106 "The Women's Rights Convention."

106 "The Women's Rights Convention."

106 Kaminski, *Dr. Mary Walker's Civil War*, 218.

106 Harris, *Dr. Mary Walker*, 110.

106 Harris, 110.

106 Harris, 110.

106–107 "National Women's Suffrage Convention," *Independent*, January 23, 1869.

107 "15th Amendment to the Constitution of the United States, Right to Vote Not Denied by Race," National Constitution Center, accessed May 20, 2022, https://constitutioncenter.org/interactive-constitution/amendment/amendment-xv.

108 "The Dress Reformers," *New York Herald*, April 30, 1869.

108 "The Dress Reformers."

109 Kaminski, *Dr. Mary Walker's Civil War*, 227.

109 Kaminski, 202.

110 Kaminski, 229.

110 Mary Edwards Walker to Mary Reed, December 16, 1869, Mary Edwards Walker Papers, Special Collections Research Center, University Archives, Syracuse University Library.

112 Petula Dvorak, "Attacking Saloons with a Hatchet, Carry Nation Helped Get America into Rehab 100 Years Ago," *Washington Post*, January 16, 2019, https://www.washingtonpost.com/history/2019/01/16/attacking-saloons-with-hatchet-carrie-nation-helped-get-america-into-rehab-years-ago/.

113 Kaminski, *Dr. Mary Walker's Civil War*, 231.

113 Kaminski, 231.

114 Kaminski, 231.

114 Harris, *Dr. Mary Walker*, 123.

116 "Dr. Mary Walker Interviewed," *New Orleans Republican*, March 20, 1870.

116–117 "Dr. Mary Walker Interviewed."

117 "Dr. Mary Walker Interviewed."

117 "Dr. Mary Walker Interviewed."

117 "Dr. Mary Walker Interviewed."

117 "Dr. Mary Walker Interviewed."

117 Harris, *Dr. Mary Walker*, 124.

117 Harris, 124.

117 Harris, 124.

118 Albert Miller, poem, *Independence* (Missouri) *Sentinel*, repr., *New Orleans Times–Picayune*, February 23, 1870.

119 Walker, *Hit*, xvii.

120 Walker, 36.

120 Walker, 39.

120 Walker, 61–62.

120–121 Walker, 89.

121 Walker, 165–166.

121 Walker, 121.

121 Walker, 127.

122 Harris, *Dr. Mary Walker*, 135.

122 Harris, 135.

124 Harris, 138.

124 Harris, 138.

124 Harris, 139.

124 Harris, 139.

126 Harris, 141.

126 Kaminski, *Dr. Mary Walker's Civil War*, 243.

127 Mary Edwards Walker, "Crowning Constitutional Argument, Oswego, N.Y., 1907." Special Collections Research Center, University Archives, Syracuse University Libraries.

127 Kaminski, *Dr. Mary Walker's Civil War*, 245.

128 Kaminski, 245.

128 Harris, *Dr. Mary Walker*, 142.

129 *Hartford Courant*, July 11, 1873.

130 Harris, *Dr. Mary Walker*, 148.

130 Harris, 148.

130 Kaminski, *Dr. Mary Walker's Civil War*, 248.

130 Kaminski, 248.

130 Kaminski, 249.

130 Kaminski, 249.

131 Julia Ward Howe, *Atlanta Constitution*, January 13, 1876.

132 Mallory Drover, "Fashion Crimes: The Rabbit Hole of Criminalized Cross-Dressing in US History," Antioch Engaged, accessed May 20, 2022, https://co-op .antiochcollege.edu/fashion-crimes-the-rabbit-hole-of -criminalized-cross-dressing-in-us-history/.

132 Alicia Deleon-Torres, "Businesswoman Has Become a Leader in the San Diego LGBTQ Community," *San Diego Union-Tribune*, July 29, 2020.

132 German Lopez, "'Walking While Trans': How Transgender Women of Color Are Profiled," Vox.com, July 21, 2015.

133 Elizabeth Cady Stanton, Susan B. Anthony, and Matilda Joslyn Gage, eds., *History of Woman Suffrage*, vol. 3, 1876–1885 (Salem, NH: Ayers, 1985), 31.

134 "A Reckless Dog," *New York Times*, September 7, 1876.

134 "A Reckless Dog."

134 "A Reckless Dog."

134 Harris, *Dr. Mary Walker*, 151.

135 Kaminski, *Dr. Mary Walker's Civil War*, 252.

135 Harris, *Dr. Mary Walker*, 151.

135 Harris, 152.

136 "Social and Political," *Hartford Courant*, March 24, 1877.

136 Mary Edwards Walker [A Woman Physician and Surgeon, pseud.], *Unmasked, or the Science of Immorality* (Philadelphia: Wm. H. Boyd, 1878), 1.

136 Walker, 1.

138 Walker, 38.

138 Walker, 50.

138 Walker, 34.

138 Walker, 145.

139 "Dr. Alvah Walker," Find a Grave, accessed May 20, 2022, https://www.findagrave.com/memorial/26017603/alvah -walker.

140 Harris, *Dr. Mary Walker*, 169.

140 Harris, 169.

141 "Dr. Mary Walker's Vote," *Oswego (NY) Palladium*, November 4, 1880.

141 "Dr. Mary Walker's Vote."

141 "Dr. Mary E. Walker and Her Mother," *Milwaukee Daily Sentinel*, January 13, 1881.

141 "Dr. Mary E. Walker and Her Mother."

142 "A New Applicant," *New York Times*, June 26, 1881.

143 Harris, *Dr. Mary Walker*, 173.

143 Harris, 173.

143 Snyder, *Dr. Mary Walker: The Little Lady in Pants*, 117.

144 Snyder, 118.

145 Charlotte Perkins Gilman, *The Diaries of Charlotte Perkins Gilman: Volume 1 1879–1887 and Volume 2 1890–1935* (Charlottesville: University Press of Virginia, 1994), 355.

145 Jill Rudd and Val Gough, eds., *Charlotte Perkins Gilman: Optimist Reformer* (Iowa City: University of Iowa Press, 1999), 70.

145 Charlotte Perkins Gilman, "Why Women Do Not Reform Their Dress." Boston: *Woman's Journal*, October 23, 1886.

146 Harris, *Dr. Mary Walker*, 179.

146 Harris, 179.

147 Harris, 181.

147 Dale L. Walker, *Mary Edwards Walker: Above and Beyond*, 188.

147 Walker, 188.

147–148 "Dr. Mary Walker's New Role," *New York Times*, March 8, 1887.

149 "Appeal from Dr. Mary Walker," *Fitchburg (MA) Sentinel*, October 30, 1888.

149 "Mary in the Speaker's Stand," *Lima (OH) Democratic Times*, March 7, 1889.

150 Harris, *Dr. Mary Walker*, 186.

150 Kaminski, *Dr. Mary Walker's Civil War*, 268–269.

151 "Dr. Mary Saw the Show," *World*, February 5, 1893.

153 Harris, *Dr. Mary Walker*, 196.

153 "Why Women Should Wear Trousers," *Home Circle*, circa 1890s, clipping, Special Collections Research Center, University Archives, Syracuse University Libraries.

153 "Capital Punishment," *Boston Globe*, November 5, 1894.

153–154 "Capital Punishment."

154 Harris, *Dr. Mary Walker*, 205.

154 Harris, 206.

154 Harris, 206.

155 Mary Edwards Walker, "Reminiscences (on Mary Walker)," Mary Edwards Walker Papers, Box 4, Special Collections Research Center, University Archives, Syracuse University Libraries.

155 Walker.

155 Walker.

155 Walker.

155 Walker.

155 Walker.

156 Kaminski, *Dr. Mary Walker's Civil War*, 273.

156 "Dr. Mary Walker's Little Speech," *Oswego (NY) Palladium*, February 23, 1898.

156 "Dr. Mary Walker's Little Speech."

157 "Dr. Mary Walker's Little Speech."

157 "Dr. Mary Walker's Little Speech."

158 "Dr. Mary Not a Daughter," *Washington Post*, February 24, 1898.

159 "Dr. Mary Walker in Town," *Washington Post*, January 4, 1898.

160 "Dr. Mary Walker's Views," *Washington Post*, January 26, 1898.

160 "Dr. Mary Walker's Views."

160–161 "Notes and Comments," *Hartford Courant*, January 12, 1898.

161 "Dr. Mary Walker's Repartee," *Washington Post*, February 13, 1898.

161 "Dr. Mary Walker's Repartee."

162 "Dr. Mary Walker's Repartee."

162 Harris, *Dr. Mary Walker*, 213.

162 Harris, 213.

162 Mary Edwards Walker, *Isonomy* (self-pub., 1898), 4–5.

162 "30 Years in Trousers," *Boston Globe*, March 20, 1898.

162 "30 Years in Trousers."

163 "30 Years in Trousers."

163 "30 Years in Trousers."

165 Harris, *Dr. Mary Walker*, 223.

166 "Doctor Walker's Narrow Escape," *Oswego (NY) Palladium*, September 18, 1901.

167 "Mary E. Walker, MD, Defines Her Idea of Murder," *Oswego (NY) Palladium*, September 21, 1901.

167 Harris, *Dr. Mary Walker*, 240.

168 "Keep in Male Togs She Says to Girl," *Trenton Times*, February 2, 1905.

169 "This Man Wants to Wear Regulation Clothes of Woman," *Oakland Tribune*, May 30, 1905, https://yesterdaysprint.tumblr.com/post/151692693554/oakland-tribune-california-may-30-1905.

169 "This Man Wants to Wear Regulation Clothes."

169 "This Man Wants to Wear Regulation Clothes."

169 Kaminski, *Dr. Mary Walker's Civil War*, 273.

169 Kaminski, 274.

170 "Dr. Mary Walker Is Ill," *Washington Post*, February 17, 1906.

170 "Dr. Mary Walker Is Ill."

170 "Dr. Mary Walker Is Ill."

170 Mary Edwards Walker, *Consumptive School Sanitarium*, (self-pub., May 10, 1900).

171 Walker.

171 Harris, *Dr. Mary Walker*, 241.

171 "Offers Her Index Finger," *New York Times*, August 17, 1911.

172 Harris, *Dr. Mary Walker*, 242.

172 "Dr. Mary Walker Gives Home as Humane Prison for Young," *Washington Times*, July 30, 1906.

172 "Dr. Mary Walker Gives Home."

173 Kaminski, *Dr. Mary Walker's Civil War*, 275.

173 Kaminski, 275.

174 Harris, *Dr. Mary Walker*, 248.

174 "10,000 Men in the Ranks Join Biggest Demonstration Ever Held in New York," *New York Evening World*, October 23, 1915, late edition.

174–175 Erin Blakemore, "The Real Women's Suffrage Milestone That Just Turned 100," *Time*, October 23, 2015, https://time.com/4081629/suffrage -parade-1915.

175 Harris, *Dr. Mary Walker*, 251.

177 Harris, 252.

177 "Dr. Mary E. Walker," *Rome (NY) Sentinel*, January 1896.

177 Harris, *Dr. Mary Walker*, 252.

178 Dale E. Walker, *Mary Edwards Walker: Above and Beyond*, 206.

179 "The History of the Equal Rights Amendment," Alice Paul Institute, accessed May 20, 2022, https://alicepaul.org/era/.

180 Rosalind Rosenberg, *Divided Lives: American Women in the Twentieth Century* (New York: Hill & Wang, 2008), 225.

180 Anne Walker to Barbara Kilberg, "Walker, Dr. Mary—Congressional Medal of Honor, 1974–77," Box 9 of the Bobbie Greene Kilberg Files, 1974–77, Gerald R. Ford Presidential Library.

180 Walker to Kilberg.

181 "Mary Edwards Walker, born November 26, 1832," civilwaref.blogspot.com, November 21, 2013, http://civilwaref.blogspot.com/2013/11/mary-edwards-walker-born-november-26.html.

181 Dale E. Walker, *Mary Edwards Walker: Above and Beyond*, 206.

181 Walker, 206.

SELECTED BIBLIOGRAPHY

Enss, Chris. *The Pinks: The First Women Detectives, Operatives, and Spies with the Pinkerton National Detective Agency*. Guilford, CT: TwoDot, 2017. See esp. chap. 9, "Operative Dr. Mary Edwards Walker."

Fischer, Gayle Veronica. "A Matter of Wardrobe? Mary Edwards Walker, a Nineteenth-Century American Cross-Dresser." *Fashion Theory* 2, no. 3 (1998): 245–268.

Graf, Mercedes. *A Woman of Honor: Dr. Mary E. Walker and the Civil War*. Gettysburg, PA: Thomas, 2001.

Gubar, Susan. "Blessings in Disguise: Cross-Dressing as Re-Dressing for Female Modernists." *Massachusetts Review* 22, no. 3 (Autumn 1981): 477–508.

Harris, Sharon M. *Dr. Mary Walker: An American Radical, 1832–1919*. New Brunswick, NJ: Rutgers University Press, 2009.

———. "Dr. Mary Walker and the Economies of Letter Writing." In *Letters and Cultural Transformations in the United States*, edited by Theresa Strouth Gaul and Sharon M. Harris. Burlington, VT: Ashgate, 2009.

Kaminski, Theresa. *Dr. Mary Walker's Civil War: One Woman's Journey to the Medal of Honor and the Fight for Women's Rights*. Guilford CT: Lyons, 2020.

Klifto, Kevin M., Amy Quan, and A. Lee Dellon. "Mary Edwards Walker (1832–1919): Approach to Limb Salvage Therapy," *Wound Repair and Regeneration* 27 (2019): 285–287.

Leonard, Elizabeth D. *All the Daring of the Soldier: Women of the Civil War Armies.* New York: W. W. Norton, 1999.

———. *Yankee Women: Gender Battles in the Civil War.* New York: W. W. Norton, 1994.

Snyder, Charles McCool. *Dr. Mary Walker: The Little Lady in Pants.* New York: Vantage, 1962.

Spiegel, Allen D., and Peter B. Suskind. "Mary Edwards Walker, MD: A Feminist Physician a Century Ahead of Her Time." *Journal of Community Health* 21, no. 3 (June 1996): 211–235.

Walker, Dale. *Mary Edwards Walker: Above and Beyond.* New York: Forge, 2005.

Walker, Mary Edwards. *Crowning Constitutional Argument.* Oswego, NY: printed by the author, 1907.

———. *Hit.* New York: American News, 1871.

———. *Hit: A Critical Annotation of the Polemical Autobiography of America's First Woman Surgeon.* Edited by Eric v.d. Luft. North Syracuse, NY: Gegensatz, 2019.

———. *Isonomy.* Oswego, NY: printed by the author, 1898.

———. *Unmasked, or the Science of Immorality.* Philadelphia: Wm. H. Boyd, 1878. [Author cited as "A Woman Physician and Surgeon."]

INDEX

PHOTO ACKNOWLEDGMENTS

Image credits: Wellcome Collection/Wikimedia Commons (CC BY 4.0), p. 2; Library of Congress, pp. 6, 11, 16 (right), 30, 40, 47, 49, 52, 57, 65, 67, 71, 82, 89, 103, 105, 125, 134, 145, 148, 152, 160, 161, 166, 173, 176, 179; Index of American Design/National Gallery of Art, p. 13; Missouri History Museum/Wikimedia Commons, p. 14; National Portrait Gallery, Smithsonian Institution, pp. 16 (left), 38, 87, 142; Schlesinger Library on the History of Women in America/flickr, p. 20; Wellcome Collection, p. 22; The Illustrated London News/Wikimedia Commons (public domain), p. 26; Lydia Sayer Hasbrouck/Wikimedia Commons (public domain), p. 29; Courtesy National Park Service, p. 35; Division of Political and Military History, National Museum of American History, Smithsonian Institution, p. 61; Everett Collection/Bridgeman Images, p. 76; Collection of the Smithsonian National Museum of African American History and Culture, p. 80; Courtesy of the National Library of Medicine, pp. 91, 93, 119; Rijksmuseum, Amsterdam, p. 97; Vergue/Wikimedia Commons (public domain), p. 99; Special Collections Research Center/Syracuse University Libraries/Mary Edwards Walker Papers, p. 101; History of Orange County, New York/Wikimedia Commons (public domain), p. 107; The State Historical Society of Missouri/Wikimedia Commons (public domain), p. 111; National Library of Medicine/Wikimedia Commons, p. 115; Kahle/Austin Foundation/Internet Archive, p. 123; Bettmann/Getty Images, p. 137; Chronicle/Alamy Stock Photo, p. 146; Harold B. Lee Library/Internet Archive/flickr, p. 157; Wikimedia Commons (public domain), p. 164.

Cover: Bettmann/Getty Images.

ABOUT THE AUTHOR

SARA LATTA HAS WRITTEN SEVERAL BOOKS for middle grade and YA readers, including *Body 2.0: The Engineering Revolution in Medicine* (2020); *Black Holes: The Weird Science of the Most Mysterious Objects in the Universe* (2018); *Smash! Exploring the Mysteries of the Universe with the Large Hadron Collider* (2017), and *Scared Stiff: Everything You Need to Know about 50 Famous Phobias* (2014). She began writing about science and medicine after receiving a master's degree in immunology. She later earned a master of fine arts in creative writing from Lesley University in Cambridge, Massachusetts. She lives in New York City. Visit her online at www.saralatta.com.